Gen Tox
Live Clean!

Get free from environmental toxins, feel better, and live longer

By
Labib Ghulmiyyah, M.D.
Rudolph Eberwein, M.D.

Copyright © 2023 Labib Ghulmiyyah, M.D. and Rudolph Eberwein, M.D.

All rights reserved

No part of this book may be reproduced in any form or by any electronic or mechanical means including information storage and retrieval systems, without permission in writing from the author. The only exception is by a reviewer, who may quote short excerpts in a published review.

The information presented herein represents the views of the author as of the date of publication. This book is presented for informational purposes only. Due to the rate at which conditions change, the author reserves the right to alter and update his opinions at any time. While every attempt has been made to verify the information in this book, the author does not assume any responsibility for errors, inaccuracies, or omissions.

This book is not intended as a substitute for the medical advice of physicians. The reader should regularly consult a physician in matters relating to his/her health and particularly with respect to any symptoms that may require diagnosis or medical attention.

Acknowledgements

We would like to express our deepest gratitude to all those who supported us throughout the process of researching and writing this book.

First and foremost, we would like to thank our incredible wives who put up with the long hours and distraction of this project. Your love, patience, and support kept us going. And to our children, your smiles and hugs re-energized us when we felt overwhelmed.

We are also forever thankful for the constant encouragement from our close friends and family. Thank you for listening, providing advice, and believing in our mission to educate people about reducing toxins. We could not have done this without your unwavering faith in us.

In particular, Dr. Rudolph Eberwein (Dr Rudy) deserves special recognition for originally inspiring this project. After discovering dangerously high toxin levels, Dr. Eberwein encouraged me (Dr. Labib) to make lifestyle changes to improve my health. Witnessing the dramatic improvements in my wellbeing over just a few months convinced me of the importance of educating others. I am forever grateful to Dr. Eberwein for setting me on this journey.

We would also like to acknowledge our brilliant and hardworking research assistants who aided in compiling data, organizing sources, and fact checking. This book would not have been possible without their tireless effort. Moreover, we gratefully acknowledge Mrs. Lana Khattab Shammas for her creative vision and talent in designing the eye-catching cover of this book.

Finally, we are thankful to our readers for recognizing the value of this life-changing information. We hope this book empowers you to take control of your health by reducing environmental toxins. Even small steps can make a big difference.

Dr. Labib Ghulmiyyah and Dr. Rudolph Eberwein

Preface

The journey to writing this book began with a concerning realization: I was constantly exhausted, mentally foggy, and no longer found joy in activities I once loved. As a doctor, I knew something wasn't right, but I never expected the cause to be low testosterone levels at just forty-six years old! This surprising lab result sent me down an investigative rabbit hole to uncover the reasons behind my health decline.

Together with my colleague Dr. Rudy, our eyes were opened to the enormous yet overlooked threat that environmental toxins pose to our wellbeing. We realized our medical training had not prepared us for the magnitude of this crisis, silently affecting individuals from all walks of life, even physicians like us.

My personal mission became to find the root causes of my own low testosterone and restore my vibrancy. With Dr. Rudy's guidance, I discovered the world of functional medicine and lifted the veil on the complex web of toxins that had been chipping away at my vitality in subtle but destructive ways over time. From hormone-disrupting chemicals to heavy metals and mold, I learned how these pervasive substances permeate our modern lives, creating a "total toxic load" that our bodies struggle to process.

I began to make connections to my specialty in maternal and fetal health. If environmental toxins could so profoundly impact me, what were they doing to vulnerable developing babies still in the womb? This question compelled me not only to advocate for my own health, but for the innocent lives being harmed, who had no voice.

Implementing science-based detoxification protocols and simple lifestyle changes yielded powerful results for me. I regained energy, mental clarity, and a renewed sense of joy. This transformation compelled me to write this book and share my experience, so others do not needlessly suffer from what is truly a conquerable adversary if you have the right knowledge.

Dr. Rudy and I teamed up to shed light on the untold threat toxins pose to human health and potential. We aim to raise awareness and equip everyone with actionable knowledge to reduce their daily toxic exposures. Dubbed "Gen Tox," this book explores the mounting health crisis in today's young generation, the first to be immersed in a toxic chemical stew from the womb to adulthood, making this unprecedented lifelong exposure the prime suspect behind the epidemics ravaging this population. The good news is that with small consistent choices we can cumulatively enhance our body's natural detoxification capacity and resilience. But awareness is the first step. Our children's and future generations' wellbeing is what motivated our sense of urgency.

It is unacceptable for any person today to feel depleted, sick, or robbed of joy solely because environmental toxins have silently commandeered their health. You deserve to fully understand this predicament and reclaim your optimal vitality. Mainstream medicine has overlooked this issue for too long.

This book explores the concerning science behind toxins' health harms, but also empowers you to fight back. By sharing my journey alongside Dr. Rudy's wisdom, we aim to generate hope, practical solutions, and a path forward. You can reverse damage already done and optimize your body's defenses moving forward. A clean new chapter awaits you—rejuvenated, resilient, and thriving. But it starts with knowledge. Let us shed some light!

Labib Ghulmiyyah, M.D.

Table of Content

Acknowledgements iii
Preface vi
Introduction 1
Chapter One 7
The Rise of Chronic Illness 7
    Lifestyle Diseases 11
    Cardiovascular Diseases 18
    Obesity 22
    All About Fat 24
    The Health Risks 27
    Type 2 Diabetes 29
    Stroke 33
    Hypertension 34
    Chronic Obstructive Pulmonary Diseases (COPD) 36
    Asthma 37
    Osteoporosis 39
    Chapter Two 40
    Environmental Toxins 40
        Air Pollution 43
        Water Pollution 47

The Earth 53
In the Home 63
Building Materials 64
Persistent, Bioaccumulative, and Toxic Chemicals (PBTs) 68

Chapter Three 71
Consumer Products 71
Bisphenol A (BPA) 76
PFAS "Forever Chemicals" 78
Cookware 83
The Pursuit of Beauty 86

Chapter Four 94
Food 94
The Spectrum of Unwanted Contaminants 97
Pesticides 107
DDT 110
Herbicides and Roundup 112
Foodborne Illness Outbreaks 117

Chapter Five 122
Deceptive Marketing 122
An Avalanche of Feel-Better Pills 128

Dietary Supplements 128
Over-the Counter Drugs 131
Prescription Drugs 137
Drug Patents 138
The U.S. Drug Enforcement Administration 139
The Deadly Deception: Purdue Pharma 141
Shady Supplements 146
Marketing Strategies 149
Brain Pills and Prevagen 150
Balance of Nature's "Fruits & Veggies" 153
Phenylephrine, the Phantom Decongestant 160

Chapter Six 165
Healthy Alternatives and Resources 165

Food Marketing and Labeling 166
Organic Meat Products 175
Is Organic Food More Expensive? 176
Water, Water, Everywhere… 179
The Challenge of Recycling 186

Chapter Seven 196
Toward a Future of Clean Living 196

Greenwashing 198

xii

How Do You Decide to Embrace or Reject a Company? 204
    Benefit Corporations 207
    B-Corp Certification 210
    Fair Trade Certification 212

About Authors 218
Dr Labib Ghulmiyyah 218
Dr Rudolph Eberwein 220

Endnotes 223

Introduction

You go to the supermarket with your shopping list. Your list has all the usual things you buy every week: Milk, eggs, bananas, chicken, vegetables, fruit, coffee, cleaning items for your home, personal care products for yourself. You try to be socially conscious and health-focused, so you read the labels on the processed foods you buy. There are so many claims made! This one says its "all natural," while another says it's "made with organic ingredients." Another says it's "heart healthy." You get the feeling you're the target of sophisticated marketing people.

After going home and unloading your groceries, you turn on the TV or scroll through your phone. You see ads for brain and memory pills. Happy senior citizens proclaim their lives have been changed by a supplement that contains an exotic-sounding ingredient. You wonder, do these pills really work?

You pop open a plastic bottle of flavored water. It's really just processed tap water, but the packaging is enticing and makes you feel like you're making a smart choice. Then you toss the flimsy bottle into your recycling bin, but you've read that the type of plastic used for water bottles is difficult to recycle and billions of bottles end up in landfills. So you're not feeling too good about your choice.

In fact, you may be feeling vaguely unwell or tired throughout your day. You don't know why. You try to eat a healthy diet, but you wish you felt better, and didn't have so much inflammation, achy joints, weird rashes, and sleeplessness. What's going on?

This book provides answers.

The reality is that we live in a complicated world full of things that are good for us and we need in order to survive, as well as chemicals and compounds that are harmful and can make us unwell. Not so much by a sudden illness, although cases of food poisoning do erupt now and then. It's more a matter of chronic poor health caused by repeated exposure to low-level toxins in our food and

2

environment. We live our everyday lives and try not to do anything dumb, but the fact remains that many environmental toxins are difficult to identify and avoid.

Consider the crisp red apple you picked up at the supermarket. People often eat the skin of an apple, so the entire fruit needs to be clean and healthy. The problem is that many conventionally grown apples are drenched in diphenylamine (DPA), a pesticide used to prevent the skin of apples in cold storage from developing brown or black patches known as "storage scald." The U.S. Environmental Protection Agency (EPA) says that the dietary exposure to DPA residues in foods is "within acceptable limits." But in animal testing, DPA has been shown to cause increase in organ weights and cause damage to the liver, spleen, and kidney.[1]

That does not inspire confidence! Furthermore, the EPA says that a significant concern is the risk posed to DPA handlers, particularly workers who come into contact with treated apples following application of this pesticide. Exposure and risk to workers must be mitigated by the use of personal protective equipment (PPE).[2]

In 2012, European officials banned the use of diphenylamine on fruits, but the EPA has not. Health officials recommend washing apples with water and baking soda to remove all pesticide residues.

The old phrase "*caveat emptor*"—"let the buyer beware"—is as true today as it was in ancient Rome!

But there is hope. Our journey to better health must begin with a look at a societal problem that's getting worse—the rise of chronic "lifestyle" diseases. These are conditions—obesity, heart disease, asthma, inflammation, low hormones—that are directly linked to our everyday behaviors and that we can ameliorate with smarter choices.

Our environment is full of toxic substances. This problem is nothing new; in the 19th century entire cities were blanketed with choking coal smoke, streets were full of horse manure, and the waterways we re open sewers. But today, our challenge is that while our air, water, and homes may *appear* clean, they may have hidden poisons that can make us unwell. This book will help you spot them and either eliminate or reduce them.

Then we go shopping, and learn about which food and personal care products to avoid and which ones are likely to be safe.

In the media, modern-day "snake oil" sales campaigns abound, pitching products that carefully circumvent federal laws against false advertising. The placebo effect is powerful—that is to say, these companies count on the fact that if you *believe* a pill will help you, your mind will think it really did!

We'll explore what it means when a product claims to be "organic" or "all natural," and then look at the bigger picture of how you can identify companies that are committed to providing healthy products made without the exploitation of their workers or farmers.

With the help of the secrets revealed in this book, a healthier life can be yours! Ready? Let's get started!

Chapter One
The Rise of Chronic Illness

In our day-to-day existence, we've been conditioned by time and circumstance to take certain facts of life for granted.

We know the sun rises in the east and sets in the west. Clouds bring rain. Birds fly south for the winter. Animals—including people—are born, live, and eventually die. And as civilization and medical technology improve, we humans continue to enjoy better health and longer lifespans.

These are just a few of the things we assume we can rely on.

We think about our ancestors and the difficult lives they led. We hear about the average person living fifty or sixty years at the maximum. Infant mortality was high, and mothers routinely died in childbirth. Terrible infectious diseases like the Black Death wiped out millions of people and decimated entire continents. Disfiguring diseases like smallpox and leprosy were common. Starvation was a fact of life (or death) when the crops failed.

We look back on the precarious existence of our forebearers and are grateful that the march of progress is steady, and that with each generation, we will always live longer and happier lives.

But is this really true?

Unfortunately, reality is not so simple, especially when you look at the bottom-line, ultimate measure of our health: How long we live and breathe until we die and are buried. No other metric is as stark and as meaningful as the length, in years, of a human life.

From the time the first Europeans arrived in North America in 1492, the average life expectancy of an American steadily increased. Until 1680, it was about 48.2 years. (These numbers are an average of men and women, and include infant mortality; if you survived until your 18th birthday, your life was likely to be longer.) Then by 1780 it was up to 56.6 years. Better hygiene, more plentiful food. Until the end of the Second World War there were dramatic dips now and then (the Civil War was a bad four years!), followed by a recovery. But after 1945 it steadily increased, and by 1950 we'd reached 67.2 years. Yay! Now we had antibiotics to curb infectious diseases. Thanks to advances in medical technology, by 1990 our life expectancy was 74.9 years. It seemed like the sky was the limit, so to speak.

But around 2010—it depends on whose statistics you use—our progress seemed to stall. We had reached about 78.5 years average for men and women. After a very slight rise, by 2017 we were stuck again at 78.5 years. No progress! In 2020 we were down to 77.28 years. Was Covid-19 a factor for this decline? Yes, it was. Enough people died during the pandemic to drive down our life expectancy.

Even so, we're not making the progress we should be making. It's true that we've greatly reduced the causes of death we experienced in 1900, but instead of benefitting from these miraculous medical advances, we've developed *new* causes of death that were infrequent in the old days!

In the old days, the leading causes of death were infectious diseases. An infectious disease is an attack on your body by some microbe—a bacterium or virus. Anybody, even a person in perfect health, could be struck down. In 1900, the leading causes of death, in order, were pneumonia, tuberculosis, and diarrhea and enteritis. Together with diphtheria they accounted for one-third of all deaths of children and adults.

Other causes of death included the usual scourges: heart disease, stroke, liver disease, injuries, cancer, and senility.

By the year 2000, just a century later, the big infectious diseases had been nearly wiped out. The top killers were now heart disease, cancer, other cerebrovascular diseases, chronic lower respiratory diseases (such as COPD), accidents, and diabetes. Influenza and pneumonia ranked number 7, followed by Alzheimer's disease, kidney disease, and septic shock.[3]

What this means is that while we had suppressed infectious diseases, a new class of diseases had emerged. These new diseases have proven to be much more difficult to treat because you can't just fix them mechanically. With pneumonia, for example, all you have to do is kill the germ causing the disease and send the patient home to resume their normal life. It's like fixing a broken leg—you set it in a cast, let it heal, and soon the patient is as good as new. You don't have to change the patient's behavior other than to perhaps urge them to be more careful on the ski slope.

Lifestyle Diseases

The new class of deadly diseases that are killing us at a relatively early age are called lifestyle diseases.

What does that mean?

It means that instead of being caused by an attack from an external microbe over which we may or may not have defenses, these diseases are caused in part by *our own actions and choices*. They are a product of our lifestyle, for better or worse.

In order of their prevalence, lifestyle diseases include heart disease, obesity, type 2 diabetes, stroke, hypertension, chronic obstructive pulmonary diseases (COPD), asthma, and osteoporosis.

Does this mean that these diseases are purely the result of our lifestyle, and have no other causes?

No. Everyone has to die sometime, and there's usually an identifiable reason, or "cause of death," as medical examiners like to say.

It would be interesting if humans wore out all at once, like the cart featured in the old poem by Oliver Wendell Holmes entitled "The Wonderful One-Hoss Shay." The cart, or shay, or chaise, was so well built that none of its parts ever broke. But after exactly one hundred years of use, as the parson was driving it, the shay just wore out all at once. It suddenly collapsed in a pile of dust on the ground. As Holmes wrote,

"What do you think the parson found,

When he got up and stared around?

The poor old chaise in a heap or mound,

As if it had been to the mill and ground!

You see, of course, if you 're not a dunce,

How it went to pieces all at once,--

All at once, and nothing first,--

Just as bubbles do when they burst."

Yes, that would be interesting, if suddenly all of our parts just stopped all at once and we collapsed in a heap of dust on the ground. The undertaker would just sweep us up with a broom and take us away.

Unfortunately such a system would put all of us doctors out of business, but I'm sure we'd find other things to do.

Until such time as Holmes's poem becomes reality, we humans generally die from a particular cause—that is, one part of the body fails while other parts are still working. For example, with Alzheimer's disease and other forms of dementia, the brain is the first organ to fail. With a heart attack, it's the heart, and so on. If you agree that we, as individuals, have some control over the health of our various body parts, then you'd think that lifestyle diseases, which arise in part due to our own actions, would be a nonstarter. After all, if you were to say to someone, "If you live a healthy lifestyle, you'll probably survive until you're ninety years old; but if you live an unhealthy, sedentary lifestyle, smoking cigarettes and drinking beer, then you'll probably die by the age of seventy," wouldn't an extra twenty years of life be a powerful motivator?

It should, but it's not, because humans tend to *live in the moment*. We can't see ten or fifty years in the future. We do what makes us feel good *now*. Sitting on the sofa, eating that extra donut, drinking sugary beverages, riding in a car instead of walking—they all feel good right now, and so we do them.

Equally important—and the central idea of this book—is the fact that many of the contributing causes to lifestyle diseases are "invisible," in the sense that they're present in the background of our daily lives. These are the environmental toxins that we're exposed to or ingest, sometimes with our knowledge and sometimes unknowingly. A "toxin" was once narrowly defined as a naturally occurring organic poison—usually a protein—produced by metabolic activities of living cells or organisms, like rattlesnake venom or blowfish poison. In recent times, the meaning of the word has expanded to include what the adjective "toxic" means—any molecule that damages human life. Heavy metals such as lead are toxic, carbon monoxide is toxic, insecticides are toxic, and so on.

We'll get more into that discussion in the chapters ahead. Right now, let's explore these emerging lifestyle diseases and how they're driving down our lifespans.

The central fact of lifestyle diseases is that they are non-communicable. They're not spread by germs or viruses. You cannot catch them from a doorknob or riding on the subway. Your roommate or spouse can have one, and it won't jump to you. But you can develop the same disease if you have similar personal habits or are exposed to the same environmental toxins. In such a case, you'll be developing the disease concurrently as your roommate or neighbor.

You may be exposed to environmental toxins because of choices you make in the products you use and the foods you eat.

You may also be exposed to such toxins through no fault of your own.

For example, the U.S. Marine Corps Base Camp Lejeune in Jacksonville, North Carolina, is the site of one of the worst water contamination cases in US history. Between 1952 and 1987, oil, industrial wastewater, and toxic chemicals used as degreasers and solvents were deliberately dumped in the local storm drains, contaminating the local water supply for 35 years. Over one million men, women, and children lived and worked there, and were exposed to harmful, cancer-causing chemicals. Those chemicals included perchloroethylene (PCE), trichloroethylene (TCE), and benzene, all of which are linked to very aggressive forms of cancer. The water also contained high levels of mercury, which can lead to life-threatening neurological and mental issues.

The health issues were so pervasive and serious that on August 10, 2022, President Joe Biden signed into law the Honoring our PACT Act of 2022, which included the Camp Lejeune Justice Act of 2022 (CLJA), which allows people exposed to contaminated water at Camp Lejeune to file new lawsuits with settlements as high as $500,000.

At Camp Lejeune, none of the people who got sick concurrently were making bad choices. They were just doing their jobs and serving their country. The toxic materials came from a variety of sources including leaking underground fuel tanks, industrial area spills, and waste disposal sites. In one notorious example, ABC One-Hour Cleaners, an off-base dry cleaning firm, was found to have illegally dumped PCE (perchloroethylene or tetrachloroethylene).

I cite this case to demonstrate that the elimination of environmental toxins is something that we all must do both individually and collectively. No single person was responsible for the Camp LeJeune disaster. It was something that was created over a period of decades by many bad and unethical decisions, as well as just pure laziness. The innocent people—including many children—

whose health was damaged did nothing wrong. They just lived their lives and trusted their environment was safe.

The issues that impact our health exist on a spectrum. At one end are the things each one of us can do every day as individuals to improve our health. At the other end are things we all must do collectively on a large scale. From the micro to the macro, you might say.

Let's get back to reviewing the chronic lifestyle diseases that are having such an impact on our health.

Cardiovascular Diseases

At the top of every list of chronic, noncommunicable lifestyle diseases is heart disease in its many forms.

The term "heart disease" refers to several types of cardiovascular conditions. In the United States, the most common is coronary artery disease (CAD), which affects the blood flow to the heart. CAD is caused by plaque accumulating in the walls of the arteries that supply blood to the heart and other parts of the body. Plaque consists of deposits of cholesterol and other substances on the inner walls of the arteries, causing the arteries to become narrow over time, partially or totally blocking the blood flow. This process is called atherosclerosis.

There are three types of atherosclerosis:
1. Carotid artery disease: Blocked blood flow to your brain.
2. Coronary artery disease: Blocked blood flow to your heart.
3. Peripheral artery disease: Blocked blood flow to your legs and arms.

When cholesterol lodges in the wall of the artery, in response the body commands white blood cells to trap the "enemy" substance, which then turn into foamy cells that ooze more fat and cause more inflammation. Then muscle cells in the artery wall multiply and form a cap over the area, trapping the soft plaque underneath. This results in a narrowing of the artery.

Eventually the cap may rupture, spewing the plaque into the bloodstream and potentially blocking the artery entirely, causing a heart attack. The plaque buildup can also cause angina, which is chest pain brought on by exertion or emotional stress.

Before we go on, we need to clarify a few things about cholesterol. Cholesterol is a type of lipid (fat). This waxy substance is necessary to build cells and make vitamins and other hormones. Without some cholesterol in your blood and tissues, you would die. But not to worry—your body makes all the cholesterol you need in your liver. The problem is that we also consume additional cholesterol in foods from animals, such meat, poultry, and dairy products.

Furthermore, there's "good" and "bad" cholesterol.

LDL cholesterol, or low-density lipoprotein, is considered the "bad" cholesterol because it's the stuff that builds up in your arteries.

HDL cholesterol, or high-density lipoprotein, can be thought of as the "good" cholesterol because it actually carries LDL "bad" cholesterol away from the arteries and back to the liver, where the LDL is broken down and passed from the body. You can think of of HDL as the "garbage trucks of the bloodstream."

Incidentally, there's a new way of measuring cholesterol called nuclear magnetic resonance (NMR) spectroscopy, which gives your doctor more information about your cholesterol and your risk for cardiovascular disease. It's more sophisticated than just measuring good and bad cholesterol. This is because it's not just the amount of cholesterol in your blood that matters, but the size of the particles. Small, dense particles are more likely to stick to the walls of the artery, while large, buoyant particles tend to float along without stopping. NMR gives you more information about these small and large particles, and you could have what appears to be high cholesterol from a traditional test but be at a lower risk for disease because you have more large particles.

The key is that your diet affects your blood cholesterol levels. To lower your LDL "bad" cholesterol, limit foods high in saturated fat and avoid foods with trans fat. These types of fats raise your LDL cholesterol. Also, eat more foods with soluble fiber, which is a form of fiber that's water-soluble.

But more about your diet in the pages ahead. For now, the point is that cardiovascular disease, which is primarily caused by clogged arteries, is the leading cause of death in America today.

Obesity

In America today, the second most deadly lifestyle disease is obesity.

Overweight and obesity are defined as abnormal or excessive fat accumulation that presents a risk to health. A body mass index (BMI) over 25 is considered overweight, and over 30 is obese. In 2020, the U.S. adult obesity rate hit a high of 42.4 percent, with the highest rates in the states of the Deep South. But it's a global phenomenon, with rates rising dramatically even in developing nations.

For a doctor, it's weird referring to obesity as a "disease" because its cause is absurdly obvious: The patient voluntarily consumes more calories than he or she uses for fuel. The body then converts these extra calories into fat cells, which are stored in various places on the body, just like a bear fattens up before hibernating. Eventually, the amount of stored fat is so great that it begins to cause an array of health problems. And unlike a bear, which then fasts for six months and burns its stored fat for energy, humans just keep eating.

The best cure for obesity is to consume fewer calories and slowly burn the stored fat.

That's the simple part.

The complicated part, and why obesity is so difficult to treat, is that our eating habits are controlled by the brain, and the brain has its own ideas and emotions about what it wants, which often have nothing to do with finding the optimum way to stay healthy. Unlike toxic substances which we know are bad for us, we cannot live without food. Food is nourishment. It makes us feel good and safe. It's emotionally satisfying, especially if we have an underlying anxiety or depression.

All About Fat

To better understand obesity, we need to understand the nature of body fat, why we have it, and how it can become dangerous to our health.

Scientifically referred to as "adipocytes" or "adipose tissue," all fat cells are essentially stored energy, made from excess calories. Beyond that, fat cells are more complex than you might think. As for the number of fat cells in your body, that's tricky. In adults, when body weight is stable, the fat cell count is constant over time. A *decrease* in body weight only changes fat cell size (they become smaller), whereas an *increase* in body weight causes elevation of both fat cell size and their number. So once you become obese and add more fat cells, losing weight only makes the cells shrink, but it may not reduce their number.

There are two different ways to categorize fat—by the type of fat cell and by its location in the body.

There are three types of fat cells: white, brown, and beige.

White fat is the type that most people immediately think of. It's those large, white cells that are the body's way of storing energy for later use. This type of fat plays a significant role in the function of hormones including estrogen, leptin (one of the hormones that stimulates hunger), insulin, cortisol (a stress hormone), and growth hormone.

While some white fat is necessary for good health, too much is harmful. Healthy body fat percentages range depending on your level of fitness or physical activity. According to the American Council on Exercise, men who are not athletic should have a total body fat percentage between 14 and 24 percent, while women should be in the 21 to 31 percent range.

Brown fat burns fatty acids to keep you warm. It's primarily found in babies, because they need the added warmth and protection of brown fat than adults do. Adults retain a small amount, typically in the neck and shoulders.

Beige fat is a relatively new area of research. They function between brown and white fat cells. Similarly to brown fat, beige cells can help burn fat rather than just store it.

The location of fat cells can make a difference to your health.

Essential fat is found in the muscles, central nervous system (your brain is 60 percent fat!), and even bone marrow. Its purpose is to fuel the day-to-day functioning of the body. *Stored* fat is found under the skin and around the organs. When we talk about excess fat, we're talking about stored fat, not the essential fat in your central nervous system.

Stored fat is found in two very different places. *Subcutaneous fat* sits on top of your muscle layer, right underneath your skin. It's the kind you can poke or pinch, often around your butt, hips, or thighs. This makes up about 90 percent of a typical person's fat stores. It's normally harmless because it doesn't impact any vital organs.

Visceral fat is found inside the abdominal cavity. It surrounds vital organs including the liver, intestines, and heart. Typically, it comprises about one tenth of all the fat stored in the body. While it's out of sight, it can pose serious health risks including diabetes, heart disease, and stroke. But experts say visceral fat is easier to lose than visible subcutaneous fat, and by sticking to a healthy diet and doing regular exercise, you should be able to prevent visceral fat from building up in your abdominal cavity.

In adults, brown fat is found mostly around the shoulder and chest areas.

The distribution of fat can produce a distinctive shape of the body. "Apple-shaped" describes people with large waists and relatively narrow hips and thighs. "Pear-shaped" people have smaller waists and chests, and carry their extra pounds in the hips, thighs, and butt. Thanks to the effects of estrogen, pear shapes are often women, while the apple shape is more common among men. Doctors say that pear-shaped people have a lower risk of health issues because the fat is subcutaneous, while apple-shaped people have more visceral fat that impacts internal organs.

The Health Risks

Why is obesity dangerous?

Obesity—which is the result of truly excessive fat in any part of the body—increases the risk of many serious diseases including type 2 diabetes, heart disease, and some cancers. It does this through a variety of pathways, some involving complex changes in hormones and metabolism and some as straightforward as the mechanical stress of carrying extra pounds.

Because we're covering the disease aspects of obesity in their respective sections, let's review some of the mechanical stress issues.

The extra weight of fat-laden tissues can affect how well your lungs work and increase your risk for breathing problems. Sleep apnea happens when your upper airway becomes blocked by the pressure of the weight, causing you to breathe irregularly or even stop breathing altogether for short periods of time. If left untreated, it can raise your risk for developing many other health problems, including diabetes and heart disease. In can increase your risk of developing asthma, leading to the airways becoming inflamed and narrow at times. By putting extra pressure on your joints and cartilage, obesity is a leading risk factor for osteoarthritis in the knees, hips, and ankles. Obesity increases the odds of getting gout, a type of arthritis that causes pain and swelling in your joints.

Environmental toxins can play a role. Pollutants ("obesogens") cited by researchers as increasing obesity include bisphenol A (BPA), which is widely added to plastics, as well as some flame retardants, pesticides, and everyday air pollution.[4]

PFAS compounds can be obesogens. Dubbed "forever chemicals" due to their longevity in the environment, PFAS compounds can be found in food packaging, cookware, and furniture, including some child car seats. Research has discovered that people with high PFAS levels regained more weight after dieting, especially women. Some antidepressants are also known to cause weight gain, as well as artificial sweeteners.

Type 2 Diabetes

Type 2 diabetes is characterized by too much sugar—glucose—circulating in the blood. Eventually, elevated blood sugar levels can lead to disorders of the circulatory, nervous, and immune systems.

Insulin is the hormone that transports glucose from the bloodstream to the cells. The reason for excess blood sugar is that the cells of the body stop responding respond to insulin and take in less sugar than they should. In addition, the pancreas then tries to make more insulin, and may become damaged and eventually produce *less* insulin.

Exactly why this chain of events happens is not known, but being inactive and overweight are key contributing factors. Diabetes is associated with an increased risk of heart disease, stroke, high blood pressure, atherosclerosis, nerve damage in limbs (neuropathy), irregular heart rhythms, chronic kidney disease, serious eye diseases, skin problems, and slow healing from ordinary cuts.

Type 2 diabetes may increase the risk of Alzheimer's disease and other disorders related to dementia. The cause may be poor control of blood sugar linked to a rapid decline in memory and other thinking skills.

While there are treatments for diabetes, the only cure is weight loss and increased physical activity.

Research has suggested that two environmental toxins, arsenic and dioxin, may have some relationship to an increased risk for diabetes.

In the general population, exposure to both inorganic and organic arsenic occurs through medicinal, environmental, and occupational routes. These routes include arsenic-contaminated drinking water, typically from untested wells; drugs containing inorganic arsenic; and wine products and mineral waters that can contain arsenic from pesticides.

Seafood, including finfish, shellfish, and seaweed, can be a source of arsenic in the diet.

Occupational exposure to arsenic occurs among workers involved in the manufacturing of glass and various pharmaceutical substances; the processing of copper, gold, and lead ores; the production and use of agricultural pesticides; and the use of arsenic pigments and dyes.

Dioxins are a group of toxic chemical compounds that are the by-products of burning or various industrial processes, including improper municipal waste incineration and burning of trash. They can also be released into the air during natural processes, such as forest fires and volcanoes. Dioxins are persistent in the environment, and since they are fat-soluble, they bioaccumulate up the food chain and can be found in meat and dairy products, including beef, milk, chicken, pork, fish, and eggs. The most toxic form is 2,3,7,8-tetrachlorodibenzo-p-dioxins or TCDD. Exposure to high concentrations of TCDD is believed to induce long-term alterations in glucose metabolism and changes in hormonal levels.[5]

Overall, research has shown the diabetes epidemic correlates with the rate of release of persistent organic pollutants (POPs) into the environment. (Of course, correlation does not prove causation.) We even have a term, "diabetogen," coined in 1961 by GD Campbell of the Diabetic Clinic in King Edward VIII Hospital in South Africa. Many diabetogens are also being labeled obesogens, as there is substantial overlap of mechanisms of damage.[6]

Stroke

A stroke occurs in one of two ways.

In about 90 percent of cases, an ischemic stroke is the result of blood flow to the brain being blocked, and the brain cannot get oxygen and nutrients. Without them, brain cells begin to die within minutes.

In about 10 percent of cases, a hemorrhagic stroke is when sudden bleeding in the brain results in pressure on brain cells, damaging them.

Signs of a stroke can include sudden weakness or paralysis, numbness on one side of the face or body, a sudden and severe headache, trouble seeing, and trouble speaking or understanding speech.

They are quite common. Every year, more than 795,000 people in the United States have a stroke. Most survive with prompt medical attention, but about 140,000 die each year, accounting for 1 out of every 20 deaths.

Like other lifestyle diseases, strokes are not caused by viruses or bacteria, nor do they develop like cancer.

According to the National Heart, Lung, and Blood Institute, the top risk factors are high blood pressure, obesity, physical inactivity, poor diet, and smoking.

The environment plays a part too. Arsenic is considered as a risk factor for cardiovascular diseases (CVDs) of all types. In Taiwan, for example, arsenic levels in drinking water were found to be associated with CVDs, in particular with stroke. Cadmium has been linked to atherosclerosis increased blood pressure, and kidney damage. And exposure to lead has been identified with hypertension and CVDs, including stroke.[7]

Hypertension

Hypertension, or high blood pressure, is when the force of your blood pushing against the walls of your veins and arteries is consistently too high. This causes harm by increasing the workload of the heart and blood vessels, and over time, the force and friction of high blood pressure can damage the delicate tissues inside the arteries. This can ultimately lead to other conditions including arrhythmia, heart attack, and stroke.

The scary thing about hypertension is that there are no symptoms. Nearly half of adults who have hypertension don't realize it—and it can be dangerous if not treated. That's why it's called "the silent killer."

Hypertension usually doesn't have a single, clear cause. Contributing factors can include unhealthy eating patterns (including a diet high in sodium), lack of physical activity, and high consumption of alcohol.

Other factors can be certain medications, including recreational drug use, such as amphetamines and cocaine; immunosuppressants; NSAIDs and oral contraceptives (the pill); kidney disease; and tobacco use, including smoking, vaping, and using smokeless tobacco.

Occupational stress—a combination of high demands at work with low decision latitude or control—has been related to high ambulatory blood pressures in men.

Your environment can significantly increase arterial blood pressure (BP) including loud noises, cold temperature, high altitude, and ambient air pollutants.

What we call "air pollution" is a complex mixture of gaseous components and particulate matter. Recent studies have revealed that particulate pollutants cause significant increases in blood pressure levels in both short- and long-term exposures.

People in regions of the world with the highest rates of hypertension and diabetes—India and Asia—also suffer from the highest levels of exposure to airborne particulate matter and environmental noise. In the U.S., the Environmental Protection Agency identifies the most susceptible groups, including elderly adults, as those at higher risk for adverse health effects from air pollution. Obese people and diabetic patients might also be at higher risk of cardiovascular disease from exposure to air pollution.

Chronic Obstructive Pulmonary Diseases (COPD)

The two common conditions that make up COPD are emphysema and chronic bronchitis. Emphysema involves the gradual damage of lung tissue, specifically the destruction of the alveoli (tiny air sacs). Over time, the alveoli rupture and create one big air pocket instead of many small ones. This reduction in the lung surface prevents oxygen from moving through to the bloodstream, and causes wheezing and shortness of breath.

Most people with emphysema also have chronic bronchitis, which is the inflammation of the bronchial tubes that carry air to your lungs, which leads to a persistent cough.

The main cause of COPD is long-term exposure to airborne irritants including tobacco smoke (cigarette smoking), marijuana smoke, air pollution, and chemical fumes and dust. When you're at work and you breathe fumes from certain chemicals or dust from grain, cotton, wood, or mining products, you're more likely to develop COPD. The same applies if you're breathing common indoor pollutants, such as fumes from heating fuel, as well as outdoor pollutants like car exhaust.

Asthma

Asthma is when your airways become inflamed, narrow, and swell, and produce extra mucus, which makes it difficult to breathe. This also causes chest pain, cough, and wheezing.

According to the Centers for Disease Control and Prevention, about 1 in 13 people in the United States has asthma. It affects people of all ages and often starts during childhood. It can be a minor nuisance or it can disrupt your daily activities. The symptoms may sometimes flare-up unexpectedly. In some cases, it may lead to a life-threatening attack.

It's considered an inflammatory condition caused mainly by your immune system overreacting to a foreign substance, as happens with an allergic reaction. Such substances may include pollen, mold, and other forms of air pollution or allergens. Other risk factors include obesity and breathing in chemicals or industrial dusts in the workplace or home.

Research has shown that people living in urban areas and close to roads with a high volume of traffic, and especially high levels of diesel exhaust fumes, have a greater risk of asthma; and exposure to tobacco smoke in the home is a common risk factor for asthma in children.[8]

Osteoporosis

Osteoporosis is a bone disease characterized by a loss of bone mineral density and bone mass, or when the quality or structure of bone weakens. This can lead to a decrease in bone strength and an increase the risk of broken bones. Like hypertension, osteoporosis is a "silent" disease and you may not realize you have it until you fracture a bone. Breaks can occur in any bone but happen most frequently in vertebrae in the spine and bones of the hip and wrist.

There are many causes of osteoporosis, including a diet low in calcium and vitamin D. Excessive weight-loss dieting or poor protein intake may increase your risk for bone loss and osteoporosis. Low levels of physical activity, heavy alcohol consumption, and smoking can contribute to an increased rate of bone loss.

Chapter Two
Environmental Toxins

If it gives you any comfort to know this, we humans have been battling toxins in our environment ever since the first cave man saw a volcano and thought, "All that smoke is very bad for my air quality." Then the same cave man retreated into his underground home, lit his fire to cook his woolly mammoth steak, and proceeded to poison himself with carbon monoxide and other pollutants from the burning embers.

Later, that same cave man noticed the water in the stream running past his dwelling was fouled with human waste. "Now I cannot drink this water," he said. "My neighbors upstream are using it as a latrine. That's not fair!" So he left his cave and, circling around, walked up the stream beyond where his neighbors lived. There he found a new cave where the water was clean.

"Let them deal with *my* dirty water!" he said smugly.

Five thousand years later—say, around the year 1300 CE, when the Middle Ages was in full swing—the descendant of the cave man (for he had married a cave lady, and together they had many progeny) was living by the same stream. Now this descendant had a house and a farm, and life was good. Human waste went into a pit in at the edge of a field, where it did not mingle with the groundwater.

But one day, a leather dealer built a tannery upstream from his farm. Tanning animal hides into leather was a nasty business in which you replaced all of the moisture in the hide with tannins, traditionally made from a solution of oak bark. You trimmed off masses of excess fat and sinew, made caustic lime baths, and soaked hair-covered skins in urine or an alkaline lime solution. The work released harmful ammonia gas, and the discarded chemicals and animal by-products were simply dumped into streams and watercourses, causing serious water pollution.

Butchers and fish processors also threw their animal waste products into the nearest river. In 1397, officials in the city of Valencia, Spain, the city's officials created the Office of Malaropa, dedicated to collecting and disposing of the carcasses of dead animals "and other dead things that ill-mannered people are accustomed to throwing in the streets and squares and which bring stench and infection to the city."[9]

So now the descendant of the cave man is forced to do the same thing as his ancestor did: Prepare to move upstream (and upwind!) from the tannery, or fight them in court.

As these scenarios illustrate, environmental toxins are nothing new. Some are part of nature and we just have to deal with them, while others are of our own making. While we can take measures to protect ourselves from natural toxins, we must be more aggressive in rooting out man-made toxins at the source—especially because they're growing more numerous and more insidious.

In this chapter, we'll take a close look at the toxins, both natural and man-made, present in our environment, there are many of them, so let's get started!

Air Pollution

Let's start with air pollution and its impact on respiratory health. Air pollution is particularly challenging because it knows no national boundaries, and toxins produced in one region can quickly spread around the world.

Some air pollution occurs naturally. This includes smoke from natural wildfires; ash and gases from volcanic eruptions (such as witnessed by our cave man friend and, in 79 CE, the unfortunate residents of Pompeii); and various gases including methane, which is emitted from decomposing organic matter in soils.

There are hundreds of man-made pollutants, including motor vehicle emissions, fuel oils, and natural gas to heat homes; by-products of manufacturing and power generation, particularly coal-fueled power plants; and fumes from chemical production.

Our discussion will focus on these man-made pollutants, starting with two types of air pollution—particle pollution and noxious gases.

Particle pollution (also called particulate matter or PM) is a general term for any mixture of liquid and solid molecules suspended in the air. Coming in many sizes and shapes, particle pollution can be made up of organic chemicals, acids (such as sulfuric acid), inorganic compounds (such as ammonium sulfate, ammonium nitrate, and sodium chloride), soil or dust particles, metals, soot, and biological materials such as pollen and mold spores.

In the 20th century, smog—a mixture of coal combustion emissions, industrial emissions, vehicular emissions, forest and agricultural fires—was a serious problem in American cities. These pollutants reacted in the atmosphere with sunlight to form secondary pollutants that combined with the primary emissions to form toxic photochemical smog.

Industrial pollution come from factories, mines, drilling operations, and transportation vehicles, which release pollutants including particulate matter, sulfur dioxide, nitrogen oxides, and other toxic chemicals. These can directly harm people by causing respiratory diseases, cancers, decreased lung function, and asthma. They can also harm the environment, creating acid rain and contributing to climate change.

The air we breathe indoors and outdoors always contains some amount of particle pollution. As the US Environmental Protection Agency warns us, exposure to fine particles can cause cardiovascular problems including heart attacks, heart failure, and strokes; as well as respiratory problems including asthma attacks, reduced lung development in children, and coughing, wheezing, and shortness of breath.[10]

Overall, global air pollution has created worldwide health problems including ischemic heart disease, lung cancer, chronic obstructive pulmonary disease (COPD), lower-respiratory infections (such as pneumonia), stroke, type 2 diabetes, and a range of neonatal diseases related primarily to low birth weight and preterm birth.[11]

Noxious gases include carbon dioxide, carbon monoxide, nitrogen oxides (NOx), and sulfur oxides (SOx), which are components of motor vehicle and industrial emissions.

As we've learned in the past few decades, the greatest and most toxic pollutant in the air today is ordinary carbon dioxide. Fossil fuels like coal and oil contain carbon that plants extracted out of the atmosphere through photosynthesis over many millions of years. By extracting and burning these fuels, we are dumping carbon dioxide (CO_2) molecules into the atmosphere in sufficient quantities to upset the "greenhouse gas" balance. Greenhouse gases such as CO_2 absorb heat radiating from the earth's surface and re-release it in all directions. Normally this is a good thing, but it's now happening too much, causing global temperature to rise. In addition, CO_2 dissolves into the ocean like carbonation in a can of soda. It reacts with water molecules, producing carbonic acid and making the oceans more acidic, which upsets the balance of biological life.

Water Pollution

Water pollution is nothing new! In ancient Rome (when you're talking about the early days of environmental toxins, all roads lead to Rome!), the first major sewer was the Cloaca Maximus, which carried waste directly into the Tiber River. By the 4th century BCE, the river was so polluted with human and animal waste of all types (including the occasional victim of assassination), the Romans had to build their famous aqueducts to obtain clean drinking water. Even today, the Tiber is not clean, and empties into the port of Ostia, notorious for its water pollution. But at least Rome had a well-developed sewer system; one-hundred fifty miles to the south in Pompeii, household latrines drained directly into the public street, which itself functioned like a sewer. Stepping stones were installed so that people could cross the street without getting their feet soiled by human and animal excrement.

In America today, while sewage is generally well controlled, nearly half of America's rivers and streams and more than one-third of our lakes are sufficiently polluted to be unfit for swimming, fishing, and drinking. According to the EPA, the leading type of contamination in these freshwater sources is nutrient pollution, which includes nitrates and phosphates. While plants and animals need these nutrients to grow, farm waste and fertilizer runoff have made them a major water pollutant. Toxins also come from municipal and industrial waste discharges, and you can't forget all the random junk that businesses and individuals dump directly into our nation's waterways.

Our municipal drinking water systems run the gamut from reasonably safe to downright toxic. The plight of residents in Flint, Michigan, where misguided cost-cutting measures, aging water infrastructure, and a dose of old-fashioned systemic racism created a contamination crisis, revealed the dangers of lead, chemicals, and other industrial pollutants in our tap water. Flint is just an extreme example of a problem involving much more than lead, as many of our water supplies are contaminated by a wide range of chemical pollutants from heavy metals such as mercury and arsenic to pesticides and nitrate fertilizers.

A new threat that has emerged in the 21st century is groundwater pollution from the practice of hydraulic fracturing, or fracking. Put simply, it involves injecting a water/chemical solution at high pressure into subterranean rocks and boreholes, so as to force open existing fissures and extract oil or gas that is inaccessible or too expensive to extract by ordinary drilling. Along with fracking came the innovation of horizontal drilling, which increases the potential of each well because it can reach more formations of shale rock that contain oil and gas. The method has been profitably used in more than thirty U.S. states and is particularly widespread in North Dakota, Pennsylvania, and Texas. It's expanding into new states including California, New Mexico, and Nevada.

Fracking not only uses huge amounts of water that could serve other purposes, but also risks polluting groundwater. A 2016 EPA analysis found that fracking operations can—and do—affect drinking water resources. The activities that pose the biggest threats include:

- Injection of hydraulic fracturing fluids into wells with inadequate mechanical integrity, allowing gases or liquids to move to groundwater resources;

- Injection of hydraulic fracturing fluids directly into groundwater resources;

- Discharge of inadequately treated hydraulic fracturing wastewater to surface water; and

- Disposal or storage of hydraulic fracturing wastewater in unlined pits resulting in contamination of groundwater resources.[12]

In addition to potential groundwater contamination from chemicals leaking into aquifers during the fracking process is the problem of the billions of gallons of wastewater. This is a hazardous mixture of flowback (used fracking fluid), produced water (naturally occurring water that is released with the oil and gas), and naturally occurring contaminants including salts, heavy metals, toxic hydrocarbons such as benzene, and even radioactive materials such as uranium. This wastewater can enter and contaminate groundwater sources in many ways: from a leaking pipeline, leaking open storage pit, or when poorly treated by wastewater treatment facilities. Even the recycling of wastewater can generate more concentrated waste products.

While fracking is still a relatively new technology, evidence is emerging that links it to damage to human health. In their 2022 research study entitled, "Drinking water, fracking, and infant health," Elaine L. Hill and Lala Ma found "consistent and robust evidence that drilling shale gas wells negatively impacts both drinking water quality and infant health." They did this by undertaking a complex examination of the expansion of shale gas drilling across Pennsylvania from 2006 to 2015, during which more than 19,000 wells were established in the state. The researchers meticulously plotted the location of each new well in relation to groundwater sources that supply public drinking water, and matched this information to birth records and U.S. Geological Service groundwater contamination measures. The results showed that every new well drilled within one kilometer of a public drinking water source was associated with an increase of 11 to 13 percent in the incidence of preterm births and low birth weight in infants exposed during gestation.

"These findings indicate large social costs of water pollution generated by an emerging industry with little environmental regulation," said Hill. "Our research reveals that fracking increases regulated contaminants found in drinking water, but not enough to trigger regulatory violations."[13]

If you suspect that your water—either from your well or a municipal supplier—is contaminated by a local industry of any type, you can raise the red flag and put pressure on your elected officials. You can also get a lawyer and sue. This can work, as proven by the story of Erin Brockovich, portrayed in the 2000 film of the same name starring Julia Roberts as the paralegal who, in 1993, and with the help of attorney Ed Masry, built a case against Pacific Gas & Electric Company (PG&E) involving groundwater contamination in Hinkley, California.

She became instrumental in suing the utility company on behalf of a group of plaintiffs. The suit, *Anderson, et al. v. Pacific Gas and Electric*, alleged contamination of drinking water with hexavalent chromium. Between 1952 and 1966, PG&E used the chemical in a cooling tower system to fight corrosion, discharging the waste water to unlined ponds at the site, which then percolated into the groundwater.

The case was settled in 1996 for $333 million, the largest such settlement ever paid in United States history to that date.

Cleanup is expensive and takes a very long time! In 2019, average levels of hexavalent chromium in water from wells in Hinkley were still peaking at over 1,000 parts per billion, which was 100 times California's maximum contaminant level for the compound. In 2021, PG&E said that they had cleaned up 70 percent of the contamination. That would leave 30 percent still there. As for Hinckley, in the year 2000 the population was about 1,900 people. It has since dwindled to about 750, and has been described as a "ghost town."[14]

The Earth

In the late 1890s, William T. Love was a man with a vision.

Having made his fortune as a railroad entrepreneur, he saw the opportunity for a grand new project along the Niagara River, which connected Lake Erie to Lake Ontario in western New York. At location about five miles east, or upriver, from Niagara Falls, he envisioned digging a wide canal, starting from the northern bank of the Niagara River and pointing straight north, towards Lake Ontario. The roughly thirty-mile waterway would connect the Niagara River with Lake Ontario and, among other services, be used to generate electricity. He planned a "model industrial city" whose growing economy would be tied to the waterway. He created urban plans for parks, community centers, roads, and neighborhoods that would encompass what he had grandly named Love Canal.

In May 1894, work on the canal began. From steel companies and other manufacturers, Love garnered interest in opening plants along the canal, and he managed to build a few streets and houses.

The financial Panic of 1893 stalled the project. It was permanently derailed in 1906, when environmental lobbyists convinced Congress to pass a law that prohibited the diversion of any water out of the Niagara River. The goal was to preserve the beautiful falls, which were becoming a big tourist attraction. When Love was forced to abandon it, the Love Canal had been dug out for about a mile in length, but not yet connected to the river. All that was left to commemorate Love's dream was huge dry ditch.

The last piece of property owned by Love's corporation was sold at public auction in 1910. The canal gradually filled with water. Local children swam there during summers and skated during the winters.

In the 1920s, the city of Niagara Falls began to use the giant ditch as a municipal landfill. Industry was booming in the area, and in the early 1940s, Hooker Chemical Company began searching for a place to dispose of large quantities of chemical waste. In 1942, the Niagara Power and Development Company granted permission to Hooker to dump its waste directly into the canal. The water was drained and the canal bed lined with thick clay. Hooker then began depositing 55-gallon drums of industrial waste. Five years later, Hooker bought the entire site, as well as the 70-foot-wide banks on either side of the canal. This eventually became 16-acre landfill.

In early 1952, the Niagara Falls City School District proposed the site be used for a new school to serve the growing community. (Yes, this really happened!) Hooker saw an opportunity to unload a potential liability. Bjarne Klaussen, Hooker's vice president, wrote to the company president, R.L. Murray, suggesting that the sale could shield the company from future liabilities caused by the toxic chemicals:

"The more we thought about it, the more interested [legal counsel Ainsley] Wilcox and I became in the proposition, and finally came to the conclusion that the Love Canal property is rapidly becoming a liability because of housing projects in the near vicinity of our property. A school, however, could be built in the center unfilled section (with chemicals underground). We became convinced that it would be a wise move to turn this property over to the schools provided we could not be held responsible for future claims or damages resulting from underground storage of chemicals."[15]

With the school district pressuring Hooker to sell, the company ceased using Love Canal as a dumpsite. During a decade of operations, it had served as the dumping site of 21,800 short tons of toxic chemicals, including solvents for rubber and synthetic resins, caustics, perfumes, alkalines, and fatty acid and chlorinated hydrocarbons resulting from the manufacturing of dyes. The barrels of chemicals were buried at a depth of twenty to twenty-five feet. Hooker covered them with dirt and a clay seal to prevent leakage. It wasn't long before scrubby vegetation began to grow atop the dump site.

In 1955, the new school opened, with 400 children attending. When it rained, puddles of toxic water formed that children enjoyed playing in. Then a second school was opened six blocks away. The school district sold the remaining land to private developers for new home construction and to the Niagara Falls Housing Authority. An attorney for Hooker, Arthur Chambers, warned the land was not suitable for construction. A sewer system was built, resulting in the breaching of the clay barrier and the leakage of chemicals.

By the 1970s, Love Canal was a vibrant, prosperous community with 800 houses, 240 low-income apartments, and over 400 children enrolled in school. The persistent smell of chemicals in the air and the sight of colored water in puddles did not concern city authorities.

In 1977, a harsh winter storm dumped nearly four feet of snow on the ground. As it melted, the excess water raised the water table and chemicals began seeping into the basements of homes. That spring, the State Departments of Health and Environmental Conservation began an intensive soil, air, and groundwater sampling and analysis program. Data from the basements of numerous homes in the first ring directly adjacent to the Love Canal showed high levels of toxic vapors associated with more than 80 compounds. Eventually, laboratory analyses of soil and sediment samples from the Love Canal indicated the presence of more than 200 distinct organic chemical compounds. Some included benzene, chloroform, toluene, dioxin, and various kinds of PCBs.

On the first day of August, 1978, the headline of a front-page story in *The New York Times* blared:

UPSTATE WASTE SITE MAY ENDANGER LIVES

"NIAGARA FALLS, N.Y., Aug. 1—Twenty-five years after the Hooker Chemical Company stopped using the Love Canal here as an industrial dump, 82 different compounds, 11 of them suspected carcinogens, have begun percolating upward through the soil, their drum containers rotting and leeching their contents into the backyards and basements of 100 homes and a public school built on the banks of the canal.

"Children and dogs have received chemical burns playing on the canal site, and large numbers of miscarriages and birth defects have been found among residents of the homes along the site."[16]

As Eckardt C. Beck wrote for the *EPA Journal*, "I visited the canal area at that time. Corroding waste-disposal drums could be seen breaking up through the grounds of backyards. Trees and gardens were turning black and dying. One entire swimming pool had been popped up from its foundation, afloat now on a small sea of chemicals. Puddles of noxious substances were pointed out to me by the residents. Some of these puddles were in their yards, some were in their basements, others yet were on the school grounds. Everywhere the air had a faint, choking smell. Children returned from play with burns on their hands and faces."[17]

In 1978, President Jimmy Carter declared a state of emergency, and eventually over 900 families were relocated. The total cost for relocation of all the families was $17 million.

And then there were the diseases. A study conducted by the Love Canal Homeowners Association in 1979 found increases among residents in the rates of nervous breakdowns, hyperactivity, miscarriages, still births, epilepsy, crib deaths, and urinary tract disorders. Miscarriages were found to have increased 300 percent, and most occurred in women who lived in the historically "wet" areas. From 1974 to 1978, an astounding 56 percent of the children in the Love Canal neighborhood were born with birth defects including mental retardation, double rows of teeth, and even three ears. There were almost three times as many defects in historically wet areas.[18]

In 1982, evacuated homes were demolished. The debris was buried under the Love Canal landfill cap, a barrier between the contaminated material and the surface. The disaster led to the enactment of federal legislation designed to manage the disposal of hazardous wastes throughout the country. Titled the Comprehensive Environmental Response, Compensation and Liability Act (CERCLA) of 1980, it's commonly referred to as the Superfund law. In September 1983, the EPA officially placed Love Canal on the Superfund program's first ever National Priorities List (NPL), which is the list of sites of national priority among the known releases or threatened releases of hazardous substances, pollutants, or contaminants throughout the United States and its territories. As of September 2023, there were 1,336 sites on the list.

The Superfund legislation allows the EPA to clean up contaminated sites while compelling the parties responsible for the contamination to either do the cleanup or reimburse the government for its cleanup work. When there is no identifiable responsible party, Superfund gives EPA the funds and authority to clean up contaminated sites. Superfund's goals are to:

- Protect human health and the environment by cleaning up contaminated sites;

- Make responsible parties pay for cleanup work;

- Involve communities in the Superfund process; and

- Return Superfund sites to productive use.[19]

After years of cleanup at a cost of $400 million, Love Canal was taken off the Superfund list on September 30, 2004.

Contamination of the earth is sadly not uncommon. As of August 2022, there were 1,329 Superfund sites on the National Priorities List in the United States. New Jersey, California, and Pennsylvania have the most sites. New incidents happen on a regular basis.

On the evening of February 3, 2023, thirty-eight cars of a Norfolk Southern freight train carrying hazardous materials derailed in East Palestine, Ohio. Several railcars burned for more than two days, with emergency crews then conducting a controlled burn of several railcars, which released hydrogen chloride and phosgene into the air. As a result, residents within a 1-mile (1.6-kilometer) radius were evacuated, and an emergency response was initiated from agencies in Ohio, Pennsylvania, West Virginia, and Virginia.

In the Home

When we build a new home, we trust that the products used in its construction are safe and won't present a danger to our health.

When we buy an old home, we assume it's been inspected and that any old contaminants such as lead and asbestos have been removed.

In everyday life, we trust the products we buy from the supermarket are safe; and if we know they're toxic, we assume that if we use them according to the directions provided by the manufacturer they won't make us unwell.

The reality is much more worrisome. At home, many of us are living with a higher level of toxic substances than we can imagine.

In the following discussion, you'll hear a lot about *volatile organic compounds* (VOCs). These form a group of chemicals that can vaporize into air. VOCs are in thousands of household products, including paint, varnish, wax, and various cleaning, degreasing, and cosmetic products. Exposure to VOC vapors can cause a variety of adverse health effects including headaches and loss of coordination; nausea; eye, nose, and throat irritation; and damage to the liver, kidneys, or central nervous system. Some VOCs are suspected or proven carcinogens.

They present a particular threat to homeowners and apartment dwellers because indoor concentrations of VOCs are up to ten times higher than outdoors.

Building Materials

In the old days, building materials for the frame and outside shell—steel, stone, brick, wood, plaster—may have been hazardous to make or transport, but at least when they got into your home they were inert and didn't give off weird chemicals that could make you unwell. The interior of the home was a different story, and old houses can be full of nasty stuff like asbestos, lead paint, and polychlorinated biphenyls (PCBs).

While progress has been made to eradicate those toxins, new problems are emerging as manufacturers seek to create cheaper, more durable materials using the miracle of modern chemistry. Many of these materials give off toxic gases over time. Materials that "offgas" include drywall glues, spray insulation foam, sheet vinyl flooring, rubber flooring, nylon carpeting, epoxy coatings while curing, glues used in flooring, medium density fiberboard (MDF) that gives off formaldehyde, many laminate countertops, and furnishings with flame retardants.

If you have wall-to-wall carpet, you'll want to know that the "new carpet smell" may not be good for you. Carpet backing is commonly made with a synthetic rubber derived from styrene and butadiene, both of which are respiratory irritants even at low levels of exposure. With long-term exposure it gets worse: high levels of styrene are associated with nerve damage, and butadiene is associated with cancer and heart disease. The list of chemicals used in synthetic carpeting includes many known and suspected carcinogens including formaldehyde and benzene, as well as other volatile organic compounds (VOCs).

Part of the problem with carpeting is that due to the lack of transparency in the carpet industry, it's extremely difficult to identify all the materials used in every sample of carpet. Homeowners have little choice but to trust product reviews and salespeople for guidance as to which carpets are the safest.

Flame retardant and flame resistant fabrics are common today. A fabric that is flame retardant has been treated with chemicals that slow the speed of burning, while a flame resistant fabric has been treated with chemicals that make it less likely to catch fire in the first place.

Both treatments require chemicals sprayed or otherwise applied to fabrics, furniture, electronics, and building materials intended to help prevent fires. Despite the claims of the chemical industry, many of these treatments are unnecessary, don't work very well, and are toxic. Flame retardants have been shown to cause cancer, hormone disruption, and neurological damage.

Chemicals belonging to a family of brominated flame retardants (BFRs) are added to plastics, foam, and fabrics. But because they are volatile and not chemically bound to the material, these molecules escape into the general environment. They resist degradation and enter the food chain, where they are dispersed through the human population.

If you're interested, the only fiber material that, untreated by any chemical, will not burn, is ordinary wool. Yep, it's the ancient stuff we get from sheep. Wool is naturally flame resistant, and when it does ignite, it does not melt, drip, or stick to the skin when it burns, like synthetic fabrics do.

Wool's natural resistance to fire comes from its high nitrogen and water content, requiring higher levels of oxygen in the surrounding environment in order to ignite. Wool may burn if subjected to a significantly powerful heat source, but usually only smolders and then goes out if the heat is removed. Wool textiles are used widely in personal protective equipment (PPE) to protect fire fighters, military personnel, and anyone else exposed to explosives or fire. Its characteristic of only smoldering and not melting or dripping onto skin can itself be a lifesaver.

Wool's fire-resistant properties make it an ideal fiber for interior furnishings including curtains, carpets, bedding, and upholstery, which helps to reduce the risk of fire spreading within a house or other building.

Persistent, Bioaccumulative, and Toxic Chemicals (PBTs)

To make it worse, flame retardants bioaccumulate in humans. This means they get stored in the body—particularly in fat cells—causing long-term chronic health problems as cells contain increasing amounts of these toxic chemicals. There's a name for such toxins—"persistent, bioaccumulative, and toxic" chemicals, or PBTs. Here's a partial list of known PBTs courtesy of ToxicFreeFuture.org: Anthracene, asbestos, cadmium and cadmium compounds, chloroalkanes, C10-13 (short-chain chlorinated paraffins), p-Dichlorobenzene, hexabromobiphenyl, hexabromocyclododecane, hexachlorobutadiene, lead and lead compounds, mercury and mercury compounds, musk xylene, pentachlorobenzene, perfluorooctane sulfonic acid, perfluorooctane sulfonyl fluoride, phenanthrene, polybrominated biphenyls, polybrominated diphenylethers (PBDEs), polychlorinated terphenyls, tetrabromobisphenol A, 1,2,3-Trichlorobenzene, 1,2,4-Trichlorobenzene,

1,2,3,4- Tetrachlorobenzene, and 1,2,4,5-Tetrachlorobenzene.[20]

Many polychlorinated biphenyls (PCBs) are also PBTs. These were once widely used as heat transfer fluids, dielectric and coolant fluids for electrical equipment, and in the manufacture of carbonless copy paper. Because they are persistent, bioaccumulative, increase the risk of cancer, and interfere with normal brain development in children, they were banned in the USA in 1978. Although levels are gradually declining, many people in the US still have detectable levels of PCBs in their blood.

We even have a new disease that may be linked to toxins in buildings. Sick building syndrome (SBS) is the term used when the occupants of a building experience acute health- or comfort-related effects that seem to be linked directly to their time spent in the building. The complainants may be widespread throughout the building or localized in a particular room or zone. In pinpointing a cause, the most common contaminant of indoor air includes volatile organic compounds (VOC) such as manufactured wood products, adhesives, upholstery, copy machines, carpeting, pesticides, and cleaning agents.

Chapter Three
Consumer Products

In May 2023, the journal *Environmental Science & Technology* published a groundbreaking study revealing that more than 100 types of common consumer products contained at least one, and often several, chemicals linked to cancer or reproductive and developmental problems.[21]

The largest group of products were those commonly found in workplace settings, such as factories or construction sites, and included adhesives, degreasers, lubricants, and sealants. Many more were found in personal care products, including soaps, lotions, shampoos, and nail polish. Cleaning products, particularly all-purpose cleaners, laundry detergent and dish soap, also contained potentially toxic chemicals.

Chemicals contained in consumer products can cause headaches, burning or itchy eyes, dizziness, or respiratory illnesses. Some are allergens that can trigger asthma attacks, or act as carcinogens or endocrine disruptors. Others may contribute to problems with learning.

To perform the study, researchers from the Silent Spring Institute and the University of California, Berkeley, simply cross-referenced two databases maintained by the state of California. The first was a list of products sold in the state that were known to release volatile organic compounds (VOCs). The second was a list of chemicals flagged as being carcinogens or reproductive and developmental toxicants by Proposition 65, California's Safe Drinking Water and Toxic Enforcement Act.

When they compared the two databases, researchers found 105 different consumer products that listed 33 different VOCs identified by Prop 65 as being hazardous to health.

"The thing that jumped out to us was just really the extent of the exposures," said Kristin Knox, a staff scientist at the Silent Spring Institute who led the research, to *The*

New York Times. "People can be exposed to the same chemical in a whole bunch of different products."[22]

Many of the toxic products were used by construction workers, auto mechanics, professional cleaners, or employees in hair and nail salons, who are frequently exposed to higher levels of the chemicals than the average consumer.

Warning labels on consumer products give important information about how to protect you and your family from the chemicals contained in the product. When buying a product, read the label to see if it has a list of ingredients and warnings. If there is a list, you may be able to identify ingredients of concern. There are also useful resources online which list ingredients of products.

General guidelines for reducing household and workplace toxins include:
- Use the least amount of product to get the job done.
- Avoid unnecessary use of fragrances or antibacterial products. Choose laundry and personal care products with no fragrance.

- Wash your hands frequently—especially children! Use soap and water, with plenty of lather. If you must use a hand sanitizer, choose one with isopropyl or ethyl alcohol. Avoid brands that contain 1-propanol and methanol, which is a toxic type of wood alcohol. Neither of these chemicals should be applied to the skin. 1-propanol can cause confusion, decreased consciousness and slowed breathing or pulse. Methanol can cause nausea, vomiting, headache, blurred vision, and seizures. If you're in doubt, check the FDA website, which has a list of hand sanitizers to avoid.
- Household dust might look like a fine layer of annoying stuff, but in the average house it's actually a mixture of organic materials including sloughed-off skin cells, hair, soil particles, bacteria, dust mites, bits of dead bugs, pollen, and if you have a pet, lots of pet fur or hair and skin cells. It can also contain toxic chemicals such as mercury, lead, flame retardants, and asbestos.

"Settled dust," said Krystal Pollitt, an assistant professor of epidemiology (environmental health sciences) at Yale School of Public Health, "is especially relevant for infants and children that spend extended periods on the ground where they may inhale or ingest the dust."[23]

Especially if you have children, dust your house and working surfaces frequently with a damp or microfiber cloth. Damp mop and vacuum using a unit with a HEPA filter.

- Wash new clothes before wearing them! The fashion industry and textile manufacturers often use formaldehyde, dispersal dyes, and finishing resins to make clothes look attractive on the rack. Disperse dyes are often used in synthetic clothing materials like polyester and nylon, and may be present at higher levels in a brand-new, unwashed article of clothing. These dyes can cause contact dermatitis—an itchy rash that can last for days.

- Avoid the use of aerosol spray cans. Aerosol cans were invented generations ago and were considered innovative at the time, but now we recognize that aerosol sprays are a major hazard to the environment and human health. Many contain highly toxic chemicals like xylene and formaldehyde. Aerosol paints can contain methyl chloride, which has been identified as causing cancer in animals in laboratory tests.

At least they no longer damage the ozone layer—the vast majority of aerosol products manufactured and sold in the United States now use propellants including nitric oxide or hydrocarbons that do not damage the Earth's ozone layer. Whenever possible, use pump sprays that don't need aerosol gases.

Bisphenol A (BPA)

Bisphenol A (BPA) is a mass-produced chemical for use primarily in the production of polycarbonate plastics. It is found in numerous products including shatterproof windows, water bottles, eyewear, and epoxy resins that coat some metal food cans, bottle tops, and water supply pipes. BPA has been used in food packaging since the 1960s, and it's in the epoxy resin coating on the insides of metal cans, protecting the food from directly contacting metal surfaces.

The US Food and Drug Administration (FDA) says that BPA is safe, but many experts disagree. The problem is that BPA can leach into the food. It's an endocrine-disrupting chemical that can interfere with hormone function in the body. Studies have linked BPA exposure to various health issues, including reproductive problems, developmental disorders, and an increased risk of certain cancers.

One reason people are concerned about BPA is because human exposure to BPA is nearly ubiquitous. The 2003-2004 National Health and Nutrition Examination Survey (NHANES III) conducted by the Centers for Disease Control and Prevention (CDC) found detectable levels of BPA in 93 percent of 2,517 urine samples from people six years and older.[24]

The level of BPA leaching into food or beverages seems to increase with temperature. For that reason, never microwave polycarbonate plastic food containers. While polycarbonate is strong and durable, over time it may break down from sustained use at high temperatures.

It's worth noting that because of public concerns over BPA, in 2011 manufacturers of baby bottles and sippy cups abandoned the use of BPA. It's not in them today, but the FDA still refuses to ban the use of BPA in all food containers, citing lack of evidence of danger. Their position is that while BPA will get into your bloodstream, the FDA sees no evidence that it will harm you.

To be safe, choose fresh or frozen foods. Look for canned foods labeled as BPA-free and foods preserved in glass jars or bottles.

PFAS "Forever Chemicals"

Here's another complicated chemical name that you need to know. Per- and polyfluoroalkyl substances, known as PFAS, are chemicals designed to resist grease, oil, water, and heat. Chemically, while individual PFAS vary considerably, all have a unique carbon-fluorine bond, which is very strong, making them long-lasting chemicals which break down very slowly over time. For this reason, they have earned the sobriquet "forever chemicals." This chemical bond was discovered in 1938 by a 27-year-old chemist named Roy Plunkett and first commercially introduced in the 1940s; and now its variants are used in consumer, commercial, and industrial products including stain- and water-resistant fabrics and carpeting, cleaning products, paints, and fire-fighting foams. Because there are thousands of PFAS chemicals found in a multitude of products, it's challenging to study and assess the true risks to human health and the environment.

As the Centers for Disease Control and Prevention (CDC) has noted, products that contain some PFAS chemicals may include:

- Some grease-resistant paper, fast food containers/wrappers, microwave popcorn bags, pizza boxes, and candy wrappers
- Stain resistant coatings used on carpets, upholstery, and other fabrics
- Water resistant clothing
- Cleaning products
- Personal care products (shampoo, dental floss) and cosmetics (nail polish, eye makeup)
- Paints, varnishes, and sealants.[25]

PFAS can enter the food supply through plants and animals grown, raised, or processed in contaminated areas. Significant amounts of PFAS can enter foods through food packaging, processing, and cookware. Because of their widespread use and their persistence in the environment, many PFAS are found in water, air, fish, and soil at locations across the globe. They are present at low levels in a variety of food products and in the environment, and are found in the blood of people and animals all over the world.

A study by the Environmental Working Group estimated that more than 200 million Americans had PFAS in their drinking water, and a 2019 study by the CDC found that 97 percent of Americans had PFAS in their blood.

How do you avoid exposure to PFAS chemicals? Here are some tips:

Drinking water. Most municipal water utilities test for PFAS and you can contact them for results. If you have a private well, have your water tested. If you're not sure, use a commercial water filter, which can greatly reduce the amounts of these chemicals in your water.

Food. Most PFAS chemicals in food products are used in the packaging. Reduce or limit the amount of fast food, microwave popcorn, and takeout you eat. "We know that these substances migrate into food you eat," said Justin Boucher, an environmental engineer at the Food Packaging Forum, a nonprofit research organization based in Switzerland, to *Consumer Reports*. "It's clear, direct exposure." That's especially certain when food is fatty, salty, or acidic—precisely the substances that PFAS can block from leaking through ordinary paper or cardboard. Some research even suggests that PFAS levels are higher in people who regularly eat out.[26]

It's not just the immediate use that's a health concern. When packaging is thrown into the household trash, it may end up in landfills, where PFAS can contaminate water and soil; or it may be incinerated, spreading PFAS through the air.

Fortunately, fast-food companies are responding to calls to eliminate or educe PFAS chemicals in their packaging. McDonald's will reportedly phase them out by 2025, and Burger King and Chick-fil-A have both publicly committed to reducing PFAS in their packaging.

Individual states are moving to ban PFAS. California, Colorado, and Minnesota are phasing out PFAS in children's products, and Vermont has banned PFAS in ski wax. Minnesota restricted PFAS in menstrual products, cleaning ingredients, cookware, and dental floss. Six states, including California, Colorado, Maryland, Minnesota, Oregon, and Washington State are taking action to eliminate PFAS in cosmetics. Twelve states have mandated bans on the sale of firefighting foam containing PFAS.[27]

In many states, hunters are being warned not to eat deer because they are contaminated. Because of the presence of PFAS, Minnesota and Wisconsin have advised their residents to limit the number of fish they eat.

Food handling. Choose unpackaged or minimally packaged foods whenever possible. Use reusable containers or wraps made from safer materials like glass, stainless steel, or beeswax wraps for food storage and transportation. Wash fruits, vegetables, and hands well before eating.

When outdoors. It may seem crazy, but PFAS compounds are everywhere—even in places where you might never suspect. If you've touched foam or been in lakes, streams, or rivers, wash hands before eating. Avoid accidental swallowing of the water, and rinse or shower after swimming in lakes, streams, and rivers. Do the same for pets.

In your home. Check product labels for ingredients that include the words "fluoro" and "perfluoro" and don't use them. Choose furniture and carpets that are *not* labelled "stain-resistant," and don't apply stain resistant treatments to items. Household dust can contain PFAS molecules shed from items that have PFAS in them. Vacuum often to pick up dust.

Replace or remove worn products with newer, PFAS-free items.

Cookware

Beware of non-stick cookware! In 1946, DuPont introduced Teflon to the world, changing the lives of millions of people—but at a steep price to their health.

How does Teflon work?

To begin with, all nonstick cookware consists of a coating of nonstick material over a standard aluminum or stainless steel pan. The coating replaces the layer of oil you'd normally use for cooking.

When buying nonstick cookware, you only have two choices for this slippery coating: polytetrafluoroethylene (PTFE) or ceramic. PTFE, more commonly known by Dupont's trade name Teflon, is a hydrocarbon-based material that's actually a type of plastic. Today, there are hundreds of PTFE coatings manufactured under as many trade names; some common ones are Dura-Slide, Eclipse, Eterna, Granite Rock, Granitium, HALO, ILAG, QuanTanium, Skandia, and Xylan.

Until 2015, PFAS was used in the manufacturing of PTFE cookware. The common characteristic of all PFAS formulas is the carbon-fluorine molecule bond, one of the strongest known in chemistry. Other molecules cannot penetrate or pull apart the carbon-fluorine bond, which means they can't "get a grip" on surfaces treated with PFAS, so they slide off.

Teflon is found not only in pots and pans but also in the blood of people around the world, including the vast majority of Americans.

Cookware claiming to be free of PFOA and PFOS does not mean free of PFAS! PFOA and PFOS are two specific older varieties of PFAS chemicals. Such cookware may have newer PFAS compounds harmful to your health.

Ceramic nonstick coating is made from silicon dioxide—that is to say, ordinary sand. It's converted into a "sol-gel" solution and sprayed onto the surfaces of cookware, which is usually aluminum or stainless steel, and then baked in a kiln to produce the finished nonstick cookware. The one known hazard associated with ceramic coatings is that titanium dioxide nanoparticles used in the sol-gel application may be carcinogenic and cause other health issues.

A third type of nonstick coating called GreenPan has been favorably reviewed. It uses a coating called Thermalon that is considered safer than Teflon or ceramics. However, online reviews suggest that even GreenPan and regular non-stick coatings don't last very long.

No matter which coating you choose, scratching the cookware can release millions of particles, which no one can think is good for you!

To be safe, stick with old-fashioned stainless steel, aluminum, or cast iron. Clay cookware (from good source and unglazed) has been used for centuries in many cultures and is considered safe and healthy for cooking. Enameled cookware is very safe; after all, enamel is a form of glass. Like tempered glass cookware, it's completely non-toxic and wonderful to cook with. Glass can break, but it is generally a safe option for cooking. Carbon steel is composed of carbon and iron, and both of those materials have been proven safe for cooking. Because there is no added layer of coating on the carbon steel, you don't have to worry about toxins leaching into your food as the pan heats up.

The Pursuit of Beauty

For thousands of years, we humans have been putting toxic chemicals on our faces and bodies. To achieve their dramatic eye makeup, the ancient Egyptians slathered on malachite (a green ore of copper), galena (lead sulfide), and, most famously, kohl, a paste made of soot, some sort of animal fat, and metal (usually lead, antimony, manganese, or copper). These toxins could be absorbed through the thin skin around the eyes, resulting in irritability, insomnia, and even mental decrease.

In Iberia (Spain and Portugal), cinnabar, a vivid red pigment used on the face and body, as well as for painting, funerary practices, and possibly mind-altering rituals, has been proven to have caused the earliest cases of mercury poisoning. You didn't have to actually wear it to be harmed; simply inhaling the dust as it was ground into powder was dangerous.

Men and women in ancient Greece slathered on white lead face cream, designed to clear complexions of blemishes and improve the color and texture of the skin. Wealthy Romans used white lead (or cerussa, the key ingredient in lead paints) to lighten their faces, then accented with a dollop of red lead (or minium, currently used in the manufacture of batteries and rust-proof paint) for that rosy glow.

Things got even worse during the Renaissance and after, as the "dead white" look was fashionable, and both men and women painted their faces with a mixture of white lead and vinegar.

Today, the danger of mercury poisoning comes from skin whitening creams that are popular in many parts of Asia. There is also a risk if you use counterfeit or otherwise dubious cosmetics that have not passed any tests for safety.

And let's not forget to mention the endless parades of "snake oil" salesmen throughout the centuries who peddled worthless or even dangerous substances to desperate people looking for a cure—or just hoping to feel better.

Around the mid 1880s, scientists were able to isolate the active ingredient of the coca leaf, Erythroxylon coca (later known as cocaine). In 1884, Austrian ophthalmologist Carl Koller discovered that a few drops of cocaine solution put on a patient's cornea acted as a topical anesthetic. News of this discovery spread like wildfire, and soon cocaine was being marketed as a treatment for lethargy, sinusitis, alcoholism, toothaches, depression, and impotence. Popular home remedies, such as Allen's Cocaine Tablets, could be purchased for the princely sum of 50 cents a box (about $15 today). Some states allowed cocaine to be sold at bars, and it was one of the key ingredients in the original 1886 Coca-Cola soft drink. But in 1914, the party came to a crashing halt when the federal Harrison Narcotic Act outlawed the production, importation, and distribution of cocaine.

Today, manufacturers of personal care products are a mixed bag. The ones who are proudly organic and sustainable are eager to tell you all about the ingredients in their skin creams and toothpaste, while unscrupulous purveyors hope you never read the ingredients list, or if you do, you won't care about all the complicated-sounding names. The thing about personal care products is that because you do not *ingest them into your body*, the FDA and other government agencies exert little oversight. You can put on your skin just about any toxic chemical you want.

Since 2009, more than 73,000 products made by 595 cosmetics manufacturers have contained 88 chemicals linked to cancer, birth defects, or reproductive harm. As reported by the Environmental Working Group, many of these chemicals should be banned from cosmetics, as was done in the California Assembly Bill 2762, the Toxic-Free Cosmetics Act, which takes effect in 2025. Among the toxic chemicals that should also be banned nationwide are:

- Dibutyl and diethylhexyl phthalates, which disrupt hormones and damage the reproductive system.
- Formaldehyde, a known carcinogen.
- Isobutyl and isopropyl parabens, which disrupt hormones and harm the reproductive system.
- Long-chain per- and polyfluoroalkyl substances (PFAS), which have been linked to cancer.
- M- and o-phenylenediamine, used in hair dyes, which irritate and sensitize the skin, damage DNA and can cause cancer.
- Mercury, which can damage the kidneys and nervous system.
- Methylene glycol, a type of formaldehyde.
- Paraformaldehyde, a type of formaldehyde.
- Quaternium 15, which releases formaldehyde.

According to the California Senate's Floor Analysis of AB 2762, the law forbids the inclusion of chemicals with "proven health harms" in cosmetics, "without creating intolerable conditions for manufacturer" processes. The California Assembly explained that since the primary consumers of such cosmetics are women, the 24 ingredients "risk exposing mothers, fetuses, and nursing children to substances that can cause cancer and reproductive toxicity," making it "critically important that cosmetic products are safe, properly labeled, and free of contamination."[28]

All of these toxic chemicals have been banned by the European Union and many other nations. Many are scheduled for removal from the store brands of major U.S. retailers, including CVS Health, Rite Aid, Target, and Walgreens. For example, as of the end of 2019, CVS Health has prohibited the use of formaldehyde, many chemicals that release formaldehyde, many parabens, and dibutyl phthalate and diethylhexyl phthalate.[29]

In what seems like a flashback to ancient Egypt, researchers keep finding familiar toxins in personal care products. The culprits include dangerous levels of mercury in skin lightening and anti-aging creams, which can cause nervous, digestive, and immune system damage; skin rashes and discoloration; scarring; and even anxiety and depression.

"Mercury is a hidden and toxic ingredient in the skin lightening creams that many people are using daily, often without an understanding of just how dangerous this is," noted Carlos Manuel Rodriguez, CEO and chairperson of the Global Environment Facility.[30]

Chemicals in hair dyes and straighteners are linked to breast and uterine cancer. Fragrances in soaps and shampoos have been traced to poor semen quality and fertility issues. Many American children are also exposed to toxic chemicals from a wide variety of sources, which may be a cause of learning and developmental disorders, obesity, and asthma.

In chapter 5, we'll discuss much more about becoming aware of toxic ingredients in your food, beverages, and personal care products, and then the steps you can take to eliminate such products and embrace products that are just as effective—or even more so—while using only natural, non-toxic, healthy ingredients. You'll feel so much better!

Chapter Four
Food

In ancient times, the food you ate and the water you drank was likely to be contaminated with robust quantities of natural and man-made toxins and foreign materials. Some were obvious, such as insect parts baked in your bread or fecal matter in your mutton pie. Thorough cooking was the way to make your food safe, but with things like drinking water you had to be very careful. Our ancestors knew that fermented beverages such as wine and ale didn't make you sick (the alcohol in them was a disinfectant), and by adding wine to your dubious water you could make it potable.

Many contaminants were unseen. In ancient societies, a persistent man-made problem was lead poisoning. The metal was dense and easily worked, making it popular for a multitude of household and industrial products. While many stories circulate about Romans being poisoned by using lead pipes to bring in water from the mountains, scientists today are inclined to blame wine as much as water. The upper class favored wine sweetened with sapa, a syrup made by boiling down grape juice. When the reduction was done using leaded vessels, then lead acetate, also known as "lead sugar," leached into the sapa. The sweet substance was combined with poor-quality wine to subdue bitter tannins and act as a preservative. The Romans then discovered a way to convert sapa into a crystalline form, allowing the lead acetate toxin to be produced the way table salt or sugar is made today.

Symptoms of lead poisoning include headaches, stomach cramps, constipation, muscle/joint pain, trouble sleeping, fatigue, irritability, and loss of sex drive. Sapa-infused wine has been identified as a possible cause for the rise of infertility and other health issue plaguing ancient Romans. The practice of using lead acetate as a sweetener persisted through the Middle Ages, and ordinary lead found its way into many more consumer products including wine glasses, bottles, and pewter kitchen items. It wasn't until 1978 that the United States banned lead in paint and pipes, and then in 1996 the last traces of lead were banned in automotive gasoline.

Lead is now known to be highly toxic. As the World Health Organization says, "There is no level of exposure to lead that is known to be without harmful effects." Fortunately, we now know how bad it is, and our lifetime exposure to it is dwindling.

Unlike our ancestors, we have the benefit of powerful technologies that can allow us to analyze the ingredients or components of any food item. We can know exactly what we're eating, down to the last molecule. This has allowed us to, in the grand scheme of things, to enjoy a food supply chain that feeds over seven billion humans on earth with relatively few outbreaks of food poisoning.

We hope and expect that the food we eat, the water we drink, and the personal care products we use on our bodies are healthy and will not make us unwell. We know that before they reach our homes, these products often go through long supply chains that involve many people and various conditions; we can only trust that the people who should be overseeing these processes are well trained and intelligent.

But our system is far from perfect. These days, while we're generally capable of producing safe and wholesome foods, many producers choose to cut corners and offer products that are either poorly inspected or deliberately made more profitable by the use of toxic ingredients.

The Spectrum of Unwanted Contaminants

To be fair, when judging the purity of a product, it's rarely a matter of expecting or insisting upon 100 percent purity. Even distilled water, which is boiled and condensed, is impure. Organic compounds or metals with a high vapor pressure, such as mercury, will linger in the vapor over boiling water and get condensed back into the distilled water. They can only be removed by a separate process. Impurities come from the container into which the water is placed, and heavy metals and plastic monomers are used to stabilize packaging and can leach into the water over time.

To realistically grapple with this problem, the governments of the world set standards for the maximum amounts of various impurities that are allowed in products for human consumption. For example, in the U.S. the Food and Drug Administration sets the maximum acceptable levels for many impurities in foods—including, for example, naturally occurring things like insect parts and molds. The FDA calls these "the natural or unavoidable defects in foods for human use that present no health hazard." These "Food Defect Action Levels" are set because the FDA recognizes "it is economically impractical to grow, harvest, or process raw products that are totally free of non-hazardous, naturally occurring, unavoidable defects."

Here are a few examples of Food Defect Action Levels:[31]

| Cinnamon, Ground | Insect filth (AOAC 968.38b) | Average of 400 or more insect fragments per 50 grams |

	Rodent filth (AOAC 968.38b)	Average of 11 or more rodent hairs per 50 grams
	DEFECT SOURCE: Insect fragments - post harvest and/or processing insect infestation. Rodent hair - post harvest and/or processing contamination with animal hair or excreta Significance: Aesthetic	

Peanut Butter	Insect filth (AOAC 968.35)	Average of 30 or more insect fragments per 100 grams
	Rodent filth (AOAC 968.35)	Average of 1 or more rodent hairs per 100 grams
	Grit (AOAC 968.35)	Gritty taste and water insoluble inorganic residue is more than 25 mg per 100 grams
	DEFECT SOURCE: Insect fragments - preharvest and/or post harvest and/or processing insect infestation, Rodent hair - post harvest and/or processing contamination with animal hair or excreta, Grit - harvest contamination	

	Significance: Aesthetic	

Tomato Juice	Drosophila fly (AOAC 955.46)	Average of 10 or more fly eggs per 100 grams OR 5 or more fly eggs and 1 or more maggots per 100 grams OR 2 or more maggots per 100 grams, in a minimum of 12 subsamples
	Mold (AOAC 965.41)	Average mold count in 6 subsamples is 24% or more and the counts of all of the subsamples are more than 20%
		DEFECT SOURCE: Fly eggs & maggots - preharvest and/or post harvest and/or processing insect infestation, Mold - preharvest and/or post harvest and/or processing infection Significance: Aesthetic

Sounds disgusting, doesn't it? Insect parts, fly eggs, and maggots!

But note that in each case, the "significance" of the impurity is "aesthetic." This means that the impurity won't harm you; it just seems icky. Here's a fun fact: The consumption of cooked insects is globally widespread and adds significant nutrition to the human diet. Insects are generally high in protein and low in fat, and when prepared properly are as safe as any other food product. Around the world, roughly two billion people regularly eat insects or insect products, and not because they have to, but because they *want* to. Many are considered delicacies. In pre-Columbian times, many indigenous peoples of North America were avid consumers of insects; for example, ears of corn infested with corn earworm commanded a higher price than corn without the tasty caterpillars. Today, around the world the most popular of the hundreds of species of edible insects include beetles, caterpillars, ants, bees, grasshoppers, crickets, mealworms, centipedes, cicadas, cockroaches, and even spiders.

I bring up this subject because on the spectrum of contaminants in cooked and raw food, there are three levels:
1. The substances that we think are icky, like insect parts, but which are harmless;

2. The micronutrients that are necessary for life but which become toxic in high doses, such as iron;
3. The toxins that are unsafe in any quantity, no matter how tiny, such as lead. These are the really bad guys, and most of them are not found in nature but are added during the industrial process to improve the perceived performance of the product, make it appear more appealing, lower its cost, or give it a longer shelf life.

The FDA groups these toxic chemical contaminants into three groups.

1. Environmental Contaminants

Environmental contaminants enter food (plants, animals, or fish) from contaminated soil water where food is grown or cultivated. They include:

Arsenic, lead, mercury, and cadmium. These metals may be present in the soil or waters (ocean, lake, river) where foods are grown, raised, or processed. They are often at localized elevated levels due to previous industrial uses and pollution of the soil or water. These four contaminants have been prioritized by the FDA due to their potential for harm during times of active human brain development—during pregnancy and through early childhood.

For example, the FDA tests for mercury in fish and shellfish products. The agency is careful to note that the *dose* you get is the relevant metric: "The Action Level is not a risk-based standard. Risk is determined by dose, not by the level in fish. The mercury dose a person gets depends on three factors: The mercury level in the fish; how much fish the person eats, and how much the person weighs. The definition of safe exposure is the Reference Dose."[32]

Radionuclides. These radioactive forms of elements may occur naturally in the environment or when radioactive materials are discharged into the environment from nuclear operations. Symptoms of radionuclide poisoning include loss of appetite, fatigue, fever, nausea, vomiting, diarrhea, and possibly even seizures and coma.

Perchlorate is manufactured for use in industrial chemicals and can also occur naturally in the environment.

It impacts human health by interfering with iodide uptake into the thyroid gland and the production of thyroid hormone.

Human-made chemicals used in the manufacturing of industrial and consumer products include benzene, dioxins and PCBs, and per- and polyfluoroalkyl substances (PFAS), which we have discussed earlier in this book.

2. Process Contaminants

The second category consists of process contaminants, which are created when heating or processing food. They include:

3-Monochloropropane-1,2-diol (3-MCPD) Esters and Glycidyl Esters (GE) – These contaminants can occur in edible oils such as vegetable oils and foods made from these oils.

4-Methylimidazole (4-MEI) – A chemical compound that forms as a byproduct at low levels in some foods and beverages during the normal cooking process.

Acrylamide – A chemical that can form in some foods during high-temperature cooking processes, such as frying, roasting, and baking. It does not come from food packaging or the environment.

Ethyl carbamate – Also called urethane, it can form during the fermentation and storage of foods and beverages that naturally contain nitrogen-rich compounds such as urea, citrulline, and cyanate.

Furan – A chemical contaminant that forms in some foods during traditional heat treatment techniques such as cooking, jarring, and canning.

3. *Natural Organism Toxins*

The third FDA category consists of toxins that are naturally produced by plants, fungi, bacteria, algae, and animals. They have their role in nature, but you don't want them in your food. They include:

Mycotoxins – These include aflatoxins, deoxynivalenol, fumonisins, patulin, and ochratoxin A. A range of foods including grains, dried beans, dried fruits, and coffee are susceptible to the growth of certain fungi or molds that produce toxins known as mycotoxins. The fungi that produce mycotoxins generally grow during the stages of crop production and storage. If you eat something containing high levels of those mycotoxins, or you eat something from an animal that ate mycotoxins (such as milk from a cow that ate mycotoxin-infected corn), you can get sick.

Blue-green algae products and microcystins – Blue-green algae are a unique type of bacteria, also known as cyanobacteria, that grow in water. Some are used in dietary supplements and as an ingredient or color additive in foods. But other types of cyanobacteria, including Microcystis species, produce natural toxins called microcystins, which can present health risks. If food processors do not test for microcystins, the algae they harvest could be contaminated with these toxins.

Hypoglycin A and Ackee fruit – Ingestion of the unripened Ackee fruit (*Blighia sapida*) may result in the metabolic syndrome known as "Jamaican vomiting sickness," characterized by profuse vomiting, altered mental status, and hypoglycemia.

Algal and bacterial toxins found in seafood – Produced by naturally occurring marine algae (phytoplankton), fish or molluscan shellfish consume the algae or other animals that have consumed the algae, which causes the toxins to accumulate in the fish's or molluscan feeding animal's body, and continue to accumulate in the bodies of successive feeding animals, resulting in higher levels further up the food chain.

In every case, the goal of the FDA is to reduce these contaminants to what it considers to be a safe level for mass production and distribution.

Pesticides

Pesticides are used by growers to protect their products from insects, weeds, fungi, and other pests, and their residues sometimes remain on food. The regulations promulgated by the U.S. Environmental Protection Agency (EPA) govern how they are used and the amount of residue that is allowed to remain on crops. The EPA also looks at worker exposure and environmental exposure.

Before allowing the use of a pesticide on food crops, EPA sets a maximum legal residue limit, called a *tolerance*, for each treated food. The tolerance is the residue level that triggers enforcement action. If residues are found above that level, the commodity can be subject to seizure by the government.

One may wonder…. If the goal of a chemical pesticide is to kill insects, then how could *any* pesticide be safe for human consumption or exposure?

Good question! Some people would say the only acceptable exposure is *zero* exposure. Like the FDA, the EPA takes a more nuanced view. To determine risk, says the EPA, one must consider both the toxicity or hazard of the pesticide and the likelihood of exposure. A low level of exposure to a very toxic pesticide may carry the same risk as a high level of exposure to a relatively low toxicity pesticide, for example. Like any other toxic chemical, the danger from a pesticide depends upon three factors:

1. The size, age, and overall health of the individual person exposed;
2. The toxicity of the pesticide;
3. The frequency, duration, and amount of exposure to the pesticide. Each pesticide will have its own metabolic pathway. Some, including the organophosphates and carbamates, damage the nervous system. Others may irritate the skin or eyes. Some pesticides may be carcinogens, or affect the hormone or endocrine system in the body. These affects will vary according to the three factors noted above. The EPA says:

"Part of EPA's assessment of health risks of pesticides is a determination that there is 'reasonable certainty of no harm' posed by pesticide residues allowed to remain on food. Before approving a pesticide, EPA sets limits on how the pesticide may be used, how often it may be used, what protective clothing or equipment must be used, and so on. These limits are designed to protect human health and the environment."[33]

This approach may horrify some people who don't want *any* pesticides used on *any* food product.

DDT

In 1939, Swiss chemist Paul Hermann Müller discovered that dichloro-diphenyl-trichloroethane (DDT) was a highly effective insecticide. During the second half of World War II, the chemical was rushed into production to limit the spread of the insect-borne diseases malaria and typhus among civilians and troops. It worked so well that in 1948 Müller was awarded the Nobel Prize in Physiology or Medicine.

DDT was highly effective and cheap, and after the war became popular for agricultural and commercial uses. Over a 30-year period, more than a billion pounds were used in the United States. It seemed like a miracle bug killer.

But there were warning signs. Basically, DDT was lethal to just about any animal that ingested it. As early as 1947, Bradbury Robinson, a physician and nutritionist practicing in St. Louis, Michigan, wrote, "Perhaps the greatest danger from D.D.T. is that its extensive use in farm areas is most likely to upset the natural balances, not only killing beneficial insects in great number but by bringing about the death of fish, birds, and other forms of wild life either by their feeding on insects killed by D.D.T. or directly by ingesting the poison."[34]

The EPA banned nearly all domestic uses of DDT in 1972, after the publication of Rachel Carson's *Silent Spring* and broad public outcry about DDT's damage to wildlife and people. Today, because it's incredibly effective at killing mosquitoes, use of DDT is limited to malaria control programs in some developing countries. (Interesting fact: Throughout history, more humans have died as the result of mosquito bites than from any other animal predator. Not lions, spiders, or snakes! Today, mosquitoes bring slow death in the form of malaria, West Nile virus, dengue, Zika, and other diseases to an estimated 1 million people every year.)

We are still exposed to trace amounts DDT through our food. DDT (as well as PCBs) builds up in sediment in rivers, lakes, and coastal areas, then accumulates in fish. Animal and fatty foods contain the highest levels of DDT and PCBs because they are stored in fat and increase in concentration as they move up the food chain. Commercial fish that contain higher levels of pesticides, including DDT, are bluefish, wild striped bass, American eel, and Atlantic salmon.[35]

Herbicides and Roundup

Herbicides are chemicals used to manipulate or control vegetation considered undesirable on farms, golf courses, lawns, parks, and other areas. They are used most frequently in large scale row-crop farming, where they are applied before or during planting to maximize crop productivity by removing other vegetation. They also may be applied to crops in the fall, to improve harvesting.

Herbicides are also applied to water bodies to control aquatic weeds, and in forest management to prepare logged areas for replanting.

The leading herbicide today is glyphosate. It's sold as Roundup, Ultra, Rodeo, TouchDown Pro, Accord, and others—in fact, there are over 750 products containing glyphosate for sale in the United States. According to a 2019 EPA report, each year, American agricultural workers apply 280 million pounds of glyphosate to 298 million acres.

First registered for use in 1974 by Monsanto, glyphosate is a non-selective herbicide, meaning it will kill most plants. It's applied to the foliage and transported with sugars to metabolic sites where it inhibits amino acid production. Effects will manifest in two or more weeks as discoloration of foliage and deformations in new growth. And because of its broad spectrum and (claimed) relatively low toxicity to animals, it is used in horticulture and in the control of aquatic macrophytes.

So if glyphosate will kill any plant, then how can it be used on farms that grow soybeans, corn, canola, and cotton, as well as woody plants? It can be used because in 1996, Monsanto genetically engineered "Roundup Ready" crops including corn, soy, cotton, and alfalfa. These mutant crops are resistant to Roundup and don't die along with weeds, allowing farmers to indiscriminately spray entire fields with the stuff.

Pure glyphosate is low in toxicity, but commercial products usually contain other ingredients that help the glyphosate get into the plants. These can make the product more toxic and cause eye or skin irritation, or irritation in their nose and throat. Swallowing products with glyphosate can lead to serious gastrointestinal disease and even death.

Is it a carcinogen? A committee of scientists working for the International Agency for Research on Cancer of the WHO evaluated a collection of studies and reported that glyphosate is probably carcinogenic.[36]

And as Drugwatch.com reported, beginning in 2015, people who developed non-Hodgkin lymphoma after extensive Roundup use have been filing Roundup cancer lawsuits against Monsanto and other defendants, claiming the company should have warned the public about the risk. In 2020, Bayer—which bought Monsanto—offered more than $10 billion dollars to settle 100,000 Roundup lawsuits, but thousands of lawsuits are still pending.[37]

In 2021, Bayer committed to replacing "its glyphosate-based products in the U.S. residential Lawn & Garden market with new formulations that rely on alternative active ingredients."[38]

Oh, and there's one more problem with Roundup: the inevitable emergence of "superweeds" that are naturally immune to it. (Thank you, Charles Darwin!). As Harvard University's *Science in the News* noted, "While Roundup Ready crops themselves have not caused environmental damage, they are certainly responsible for the Roundup-intensive weed management practices that have accompanied them. The environmental benefits—reduced tilling and reduced use of more toxic herbicides—are fading because the weeds Roundup was supposed to control have sprung up in revolt."[39]

This brings us to the general topic of genetically modified organisms (GMO). This could be the subject of an entire book! Suffice to say that since the dawn of agriculture, humans have been "organically" modifying plants by grafting and other techniques. For example, ancient farmers developed cross-breeding methods to grow corn with a range of colors, sizes, and uses. And in 1866, Gregor Mendel, an Austrian monk, bred two different types of peas and identified the basic process of genetics. In the 1990s, GMO foods became common, and in 2016 Congress passed a law requiring labeling for some foods produced through genetic engineering and used the term "bioengineered," which started to appear on some foods.

The big question us: Are GMO foods safe to eat?

The FDA says, "Yes."

Many scientists say, "We don't know yet."

Globally, the viewpoints are mixed. As of 2023, sixty-four countries required manufacturers to label foods with GMOs, and 26 countries had banned them altogether: France, Germany, Austria, Greece, Hungary, the Netherlands, Latvia, Lithuania, Luxembourg, Bulgaria, Poland, Denmark, Malta, Slovenia, Italy, Croatia, Algeria, Madagascar, Turkey, Kyrgyzstan, Bhutan, Saudi Arabia, Belize, Ecuador, Peru, and Venezuela have all banned GMOs.

A concern noted by Worldpopulationreview.com is that over 80 percent of GMO crops grown around the world have been engineered for herbicide tolerance, resulting in a significant increase in the use of toxic herbicides, increasing its negative impact on the environment and human health.[40]

The best way to avoid GMOs is to choose certified "100% organic" products, which can't contain genetically engineered ingredients. U.S. law prohibits genetically engineered food or ingredients in products labeled "100% organic," whereas a product labeled simply "organic" can contain up to 30 percent GMOs. "Organic" is fine for single food items such as produce.

Foodborne Illness Outbreaks

Our highly mechanized food production industry has provided us with incredible per-acre productivity of farm products. As the United States Department of Agriculture (USDA) has noted, innovations in chemicals, equipment, animal and crop genetics, and farm organization have powered increasing crop yields while using much less labor and farmland. Between 1948 and 2015, total agricultural output nearly tripled while the amount of labor and land used in farming declined by about 75 percent and 24 percent, respectively. Today, American farmers and their agribusiness bosses at Cargill, Monsanto, Bayer, Dow, and Dupont produce as much as 4,000 calories per day per person—far more than we need and could possibly consume.

Foods grown around the world are shipped to and across America. We import food from countries around the world—soybeans from East Asia, barley, chickpeas and almonds from the Mediterranean region and West Africa, corn and avocados from Mexico and Central America. The grapes on your supermarket shelf may have been flown in from Chile, the bananas from Guatemala, Ecuador, Costa Rica, Colombia, and Honduras.

This massive food supply chain also means that if a pathogen infects a batch of food products, rather than being locally confined it can quickly spread around the nation, causing foodborne illness outbreaks. In recent years, we've seen several big ones.

Salmonella infection (salmonellosis) is a common bacterial disease that affects the intestinal tract, causing symptoms including diarrhea, fever, and abdominal cramps. In 2009, the Peanut Corporation of America (PCA) was the source of a major salmonella outbreak. According to the CDC, 714 people got sick and nine died from PCA brand peanut butter. The company was forced to recall over 3,600 peanut butter products, and is now bankrupt.

In 2011, Cargill recalled 36 million pounds of ground turkey, some of which was contaminated with an antibiotic-resistant strain of salmonella. This outbreak caused at least one death and about 136 illnesses across 34 states.

In 2015, salmonella from cucumbers imported from Mexico infected 907 people in 40 states. This outbreak resulted in six deaths and the hospitalization of more than 200 persons.

Other pathogens are equally toxic. A 2015 outbreak of E. coli bacteria within the Chipotle Mexican Grill restaurant chain sickened about 55 people in 11 states. In a second outbreak for the same fast-food chain, five people became ill from a different strain of E. coli. The causes are still undetermined.

Botulism is a serious illness caused by a toxin that attacks the body's nerves and causes difficulty breathing, muscle paralysis, and even death. This toxin is made by bacteria of the genus Clostridium. In September 2023, a botulism outbreak tied to sardines served in a restaurant in Bordeaux, France, left one person dead and several hospitalized.

How does fresh produce become contaminated?

So how does bacteria get onto cucumbers in the first place? There are several ways this happens.

1. Animal or human feces in the field can directly contaminate plants.
2. Irrigation water can be contaminated with bacteria, most often with animal manure.
3. Unsanitary conditions in the packing sheds and distribution channels. These are highly mechanized processes, and one contaminated conveyor belt or container can spread the bacteria.

At home, you can protect yourself by following safe food handling rules. Thoroughly wash your hands and work surfaces before, during, and after preparing food. Keep raw meat, chicken and other poultry, seafood, and eggs away from any contact with ready-to-eat foods. Cook food to the safe internal temperature to kill harmful bacteria. Keep your refrigerator 40°F or below, and don't let food items sit on the counter—keep them refrigerated!

Chapter Five
Deceptive Marketing

Do you know where the pejorative term "snake oil" comes from?

Today, it's used to describe any fraudulent supplement or medicine that doesn't do what it claims to, or may even harm you. As in, "I bought a tonic that claimed to regrow my hair. After using the whole bottle, I'm still bald! It's nothing but snake oil!"

In fact, snake oil was originally actual snake oil. It all began in the 1850s, when thousands of workers from China were lured to the United States to become indentured laborers on the massive Transcontinental Railroad project. Among the personal effects many of these workers brought with them to the States were various traditional medicines, including bottles of oil made from the Chinese water snake (*Laticauda semifasciata*, black-banded sea krait), which is rich in the omega-3 acids that help reduce inflammation. This particular snake oil was effective, especially when used to treat arthritis and bursitis. After a long, hard day at work, the laborers would rub the oil, used for centuries in China, on their aching joints. According to the story, the Chinese workers began sharing the oil with some American counterparts, who were impressed at its efficacy.

There was a sound scientific basis for its use. In 1989, a chemical analysis of authentic snake oil bought in San Francisco's Chinatown found that it contained 20 percent eicosapentaenoic acid, a form of omega-3 fatty acid known to reduce inflammation.

In the 19th century, as news of the therapeutic powers of Chinese snake oil spread, many clever entrepreneurs wondered how they could make their own snake oil here in the United States. But there were no Chinese water snakes in the American West, so unscrupulous dealers began using rattlesnakes to make their own versions of snake oil.

A particularly ambitious salesman named Clark "The Rattlesnake King" Stanley claimed he had learned about the healing power of rattlesnake oil not from the Chinese but from some ancient Hopi medicine men. Stanley created a sensation at the 1893 World's Exposition in Chicago when, before a crowd of onlookers, he took a live snake, sliced it open, and plunged it into boiling water. The fat rose to the top, which he skimmed off and, on the spot, mixed with some other ingredients to make Stanley's Snake Oil, a liniment that the eager crowd quickly snapped up.

Stanley made a fortune. In 1897, he published a memoir that he titled *The Life and Adventures of the American Cowboy: True Life in the Far West*. A stew of cowboy poetry and self-mythologizing, and with a dose of advertising for his snake oil, this book explained how a Hopi tribe in the Arizona desert taught him the healing powers of oil infused with rattlesnake.

Unfortunately, rattlesnake oil had no therapeutic powers. Stanley's "snake oil" was just a bottle of worthless goop. The term quickly took root as a synonym for fraud. As NPR noted, the first written usage of the phrase appeared in Stephen Vincent Benet's epic 1927 poem *John*

Brown's Body, when the poet refers to "Crooked creatures of a thousand dubious trades ... sellers of snake-oil balm and lucky rings."[41]

In those days, the medicine industry was totally unregulated. You could concoct, package, and sell just about anything and call it "medicine." They were called "patent medicines" as a way to identify with the proprietary formulas manufactured under grants, or "patents of royal favor," given to entrepreneurs who provided medicine to the royal family in England. Many of these "patent" medicines were exported to America in the 18th century. They included Dr. Bateman's Pectoral Drops, Daffy's Elixir Salutis for "colic and griping," and John Hooper's Female Pills.

Americans made their own versions, and the active ingredients were often alcohol, morphine, opium, or cocaine. Available for almost any ailment, these "patent medicines" were openly sold to the public and promised to cure or prevent a long list of ailments including colic in infants, venereal diseases, indigestion or dyspepsia, tuberculosis, and even cancer. "Female complaints" were a popular target for patent medicines, offering relief for women from their monthly discomforts.

This shady industry was championed by the Proprietary Association, a trade association of patent medicine producers founded in 1881. The Association's mission of fiercely opposing any regulation was supported by the press, which was dependent on the steady flow of advertising revenue from medicine makers.

In 1905, the Journal of the American Medical Association noted pointedly that in regard to the patent medicine industry, "Sophistry, half-truths and plausible arguments are so intermixed that, to the ordinary individual, it would seem that the nostrum business is not only legitimate and honorable, but absolutely necessary for the welfare of the race."[42]

The following year, the California State Journal on Medicine characterized the Proprietary Association thusly: "This is the organization of philanthropists and public benefactors, many of whom are good enough and have sufficient of the milk of human kindness in their hearts to furnish alcohol, cocaine, morphine, etc., to man, woman, or child who can be persuaded into self-dosing by lying advertisements."[43]

This wretched state of affairs was finally checked in 1906, when, with support from President Theodore Roosevelt, Congress passed the Pure Food and Drug Act. It paved the way for public health action against misleading advertising, unlabeled or unsafe ingredients, the practice of quackery, and similar perpetrations of fraud.

And what about Clark Stanley's Snake Oil Liniment?

In 1915, the US government ordered it to be chemically analyzed. The results revealed the main constituents were "a light mineral oil (petroleum product) mixed with about 1 per cent of fatty oil (probably beef fat), capsicum, and possibly a trace of camphor and turpentine." Since the product contained no oils derived from snakes, Stanley was taken to court and found guilty of misrepresenting and misbranding his product. He was fined $20 — the equivalent of about $43 today.[44]

An Avalanche of Feel-Better Pills

While the rank excesses of the 19th century may have been curbed by government oversight, ambitious entrepreneurs still find ways to sell you products that claim to help you live healthier and longer. Today, the vast industry of substances you ingest to make yourself feel better exists on a broad spectrum, ranging from the Wild West of supplements to the tightly controlled prescription drug industry.

Dietary Supplements

At one end are the dietary or nutritional supplements that are basically processed or natural food items that you can buy in any store. In the Dietary Supplement Health and Education Act (DSHEA) of 1994, Congress defined the term "dietary supplement" as a product intended for ingestion that, among other requirements, contains a "dietary ingredient" intended to supplement the diet.

To be a "dietary ingredient," an ingredient in a dietary supplement must be one of the following:

- a vitamin,
- a mineral,
- an herb or other botanical,
- an amino acid,
- a dietary substance for use by man [or woman] to supplement the diet by increasing the total dietary intake, or
- a concentrate, metabolite, constituent, extract, or combination of any dietary ingredient from the other categories listed above.[45]

Supplements include oral vitamins, minerals, and herbal products; pills and powders claiming to boost weight loss, energy, or sexual performance; and concoctions claiming to improve memory and brain function in older adults (this has become a huge market).

These products are subject to even less regulation than typical food items. As EatingWell noted, there are an estimated 80,000 different dietary supplements available on the market today, but that's just a guess because the supplement industry is not regulated the same way food is by the Food and Drug Administration (FDA) or U.S.

Department of Agriculture. Technically, the FDA is in charge of regulating supplements, but they don't review products before they go to market. The only exceptions are dietary supplements that contain "a new dietary ingredient that is not present in the food supply as an article used for food in a form in which the food has not been chemically altered." On the label, the ingredients must be listed, just as they are for any other processed food product.

The only time the FDA can take a supplement off the market is if it's deemed unsafe or mislabeled, and this is triggered by consumer complaints or lawsuits. Anyone can create a supplement and sell it without having to register it, prove its effectiveness, or even prove it's safe for consumption.[46]

The one thing that a supplement *canno*t do is claim to cure a specific disease. That's why the packaging and advertising of many supplements includes a disclaimer like this one: "These statements have not been evaluated by the Food and Drug Administration. This product is not intended to diagnose, treat, cure, or prevent any diseases."

The advertising of dietary supplements falls under the jurisdiction of the Federal Trade Commission (FTC). We'll have much more about advertising in the pages ahead.

Over-the Counter Drugs

Before we discuss over-the-counter drugs (OTC), the first question we need to answer is, "What is a drug and/or a medicine?"

According to the FDA, a drug is defined as:
- A substance recognized by an official pharmacopoeia or formulary.
- A substance intended for use in the diagnosis, cure, mitigation, treatment, or prevention of disease.
- A substance (other than food) intended to affect the structure or any function of the body.
- A substance intended for use as a component of a medicine but not a device or a component, part, or accessory of a device.
- Biological products (biologics") are included within this definition and are generally covered by the same laws and regulations, but differences exist regarding

their manufacturing processes (chemical process versus biological process.)[47]

"Biologics" are drugs that are isolated or derived from a variety of natural sources—human, animal, or microorganism—and may be produced by biotechnology methods and other cutting-edge technologies. While ordinary drugs are chemically synthesized and their structure is known, most biologics are complex mixtures that are not easily identified or characterized.

The FDA does not define "medicine," so presumably it uses "drug" as a catch-all term. Informally, some sources say the distinction is that a medicine always is intended to have a positive effect and return you to health, whereas a drug is any substance that interacts with your molecules, for positive or negative effect. Thus heroin would be called a drug but not a medicine.

In our spectrum of substances that people take to make themselves feel better, in the center we would finds over-the-counter drugs. These are substances sold directly to a consumer without a requirement for a prescription from a healthcare professional. In that sense, they are as freely available to the consumer as dietary supplements. The difference is the degree to which the FDA and FTC regulate them.

According to the FDA, drug products can be marketed without a prescription (that is to say, as nonprescription products) or over-the-counter (OTC) if the FDA determines they are safe and effective for use by a consumer *without supervision by a licensed health care professional.* In general, nonprescription drug products can be used appropriately by consumers for self-diagnosed conditions, do not need a health practitioner for safe and effective use, and have a low potential for misuse and abuse.

So basically it's the FDA's decision whether to allow a new drug to be marketed OTC or to restrict it to prescription only.

More than 300,000 nonprescription drug products are marketed in the U.S. They have all been created from roughly 800 active ingredients in over 80 FDA-defined therapeutic categories such as cardiovascular agents and respiratory tract agents. The majority of these products are regulated under an OTC monograph, which defines the safety, effectiveness, and labeling of OTC active ingredients, and contain active ingredients, such as acetaminophen or hydrocortisone.

Unlike dietary supplements, which require no prior FDA approval, the path to gaining FDA approval for a new drug is long and expensive. In the New Drug Application (NDA) process, there are typically 12 steps, including three phases or steps of human testing in increasing numbers:

1. Preclinical (animal) testing.
2. An investigational new drug application (IND) outlines what the sponsor of a new drug proposes for human testing in clinical trials.
3. Phase 1 studies (typically involve 20 to 80 people).
4. Phase 2 studies (typically involve a few dozen to about 300 people).
5. Phase 3 studies (typically involve several hundred to about 3,000 people).
6. The pre-NDA period, just before a new drug application (NDA) is submitted. A common time for the FDA and drug sponsors to meet.

7. Submission of an NDA is the formal step asking the FDA to consider a drug for marketing approval.
8. After an NDA is received, the FDA has 60 days to decide whether to file it so it can be reviewed.
9. If the FDA files the NDA, an FDA review team is assigned to evaluate the sponsor's research on the drug's safety and effectiveness.
10. The FDA reviews information that goes on a drug's professional labeling (information on how to use the drug).
11. The FDA inspects the facilities where the drug will be manufactured as part of the approval process.
12. FDA reviewers will approve the application or issue a complete response letter.

Examples of non-prescription drugs include pain relievers like acetaminophen (Tylenol) and ibuprofen (Advil, Motrin IB), antihistamines like loratadine (Claritin 24H), and cough suppressants such as dextromethorphan (Robitussin). Narcan, an opioid overdose reversal agent given as a spray in the nose, became available on shelves in March 2023, and in July of that year the FDA approved Opill, the first OTC oral birth control pill in America.

Previously, birth control pills were available only by prescription.

The FDA provides a detailed explanation as to why it decides to make a particular drug OTC, called a '"Decisional Memorandum." In summary, for Opill it said, "For approval of a product for use in the nonprescription setting, the FDA requires that the applicant demonstrate that the product can be used by consumers safely and effectively, relying only on the nonprescription drug labeling without any assistance from a health care professional. Studies showed that consumer understanding of information on the Opill drug facts label was high overall and that a high proportion of consumers understood the label instructions, supporting their ability to properly use the drug when it is available as an over-the-counter product. When properly used, Opill is safe and effective."[48]

This simply means that the drug can be sold to anyone, in any quantity, and that no matter how dumb the consumer may be, they are unlikely to harm themselves with the product.

Prescription Drugs

At the far end of the feel-good spectrum, opposite dietary supplements, you'll find the drugs available by prescription only.

The FDA defines a prescription drug as:
- Prescribed by a doctor.
- Bought at a pharmacy.
- Prescribed for and intended to be used by one person.
- Regulated by FDA through the New Drug Application (NDA) process. This is the set of formal steps a drug sponsor takes to ask that the FDA consider approving a new drug for marketing in the United States. An NDA includes all animal and human data and analyses of the data, as well as information about how the drug behaves in the body and how it is manufactured.[49]

This may seem like circular reasoning, and does not address why a drug is classified by the FDA as requiring a prescription. In fact, the guidelines are fuzzy, and it seems that decisions are made on a case-by-case basis. The original Federal Food, Drug, and Cosmetic Act of 1938 made no clear distinction between OTC and prescription drugs. The 1951 Durham-Humphrey amendment to the act set up specific standards for classification. It explicitly defined two specific categories for medications, "legend" (prescription) and "over-the-counter"(OTC). The bill required any drug deemed to be habit-forming or potentially harmful must be dispensed under the supervision of a health practitioner as a prescription drug and must carry the statement, "Caution: Federal law prohibits dispensing without a prescription." This was the first law to specify that a qualifying drug must be labeled for sale by prescription only.

Perhaps not coincidentally, the amendment was co-sponsored by Senator (and later Vice President) Hubert H. Humphrey Jr. and US Representative Carl Durham, who prior to their careers in politics had both worked as professional pharmacists.

Drug Patents

Earlier in the chapter we discussed "patent medicines," and yes, new drug products can be patented, just like any other invention. When a drug is covered under patent protection from the United States Patent and Trademark Office, it means that only the pharmaceutical company that holds the patent is allowed to manufacture and market the drug, and make profit from it.

In the United States, most pharmaceutical companies apply for a patent while the drug is still in its early phases of development. The drug patent is usually awarded for 20 years, which would include the development phase. Once the patent has expired, the drug is referred to as a generic drug, and can be manufactured and sold by other companies. According to guidelines in most countries, including those from the FDA, generic drugs must be identical to the branded drug in terms of usage, safety, efficacy, route of drug administration, pharmacokinetics, and pharmacodynamics.

The U.S. Drug Enforcement Administration

In addition to the FDA, the US Drug Enforcement Administration (DEA) has its own ideas about which substances are safe (and therefore legal) and which are unsafe (and therefore controlled or illegal).

The DEA classifies drugs, substances, and certain chemicals used to make drugs into five distinct categories or schedules depending upon the drug's acceptable medical use and its abuse or dependency potential. Schedule I drugs are considered the most likely to be abused with no medical value, while Schedule V drugs are least likely to be abused. A list of drugs and their schedule are located at Controlled Substance Act (CSA).

Schedule I drugs, substances, or chemicals are defined as drugs with no currently accepted medical use and a high potential for abuse. Some examples of Schedule I drugs are: heroin, lysergic acid diethylamide (LSD), marijuana (cannabis), 3,4-methylenedioxymethamphetamine (ecstasy), methaqualone, and peyote.

Many people consider the grouping of marijuana with LSD and heroin to be absurd, and many states have taken steps to legalize cannabis products.

Schedule V drugs—the most harmless—include cough preparations with less than 200 milligrams of codeine or per 100 milliliters (Robitussin AC), Lomotil, Motofen, Lyrica, Parepectolin.

Doctors generally cannot prescribe Schedule I drugs. For Schedules II through V, various state and federal laws apply.

The Deadly Deception: Purdue Pharma

In many ways we've come a long way from the Wild West anarchy of the 19th century snake oil era. Now we have laws and regulations regarding the safe and transparent marketing of drugs.

But how effective are they? Somehow, people and companies intent upon deceiving us with lies about dangerous drugs can still succeed in their diabolical schemes.

In 1996, Purdue Pharma, a company based in Stamford, Connecticut, introduced a new painkiller called OxyContin. The FDA approved the new drug, believing its controlled-release formulation would result in *less* abuse potential, since the drug would be absorbed slowly and there would not be an immediate "rush" or high that would promote abuse. FDA administrators did not consider that crushing the controlled-release capsule followed by oral ingestion or snorting would lead to an epidemic of abuse.

Purdue instructed its national pharmaceutical representatives to tell physicians that oxycontin was not addictive because of its slow-release properties.

As CNN reported, in 1998, Purdue Pharma created a promotional video called "I Got My Life Back." It followed six people who suffered from chronic pain and found relief—without addiction—with OxyContin. The company distributed 15,000 copies of the video to be used in physician waiting rooms as a "check out" item for an office's patient education library. A year after the video came out, the overall number of OxyContin prescriptions had increased by 11 million.[50]

To tout the benefits of oxycontin, Purdue enlisted "thought leaders" including Russell Portenoy, MD, Chairman of the Department of Pain Medicine and

Palliative Care at Beth Israel Hospital in New York. Purdue and other pharmaceutical companies paid large sums of money to Portenoy, his department, and many other physicians to endorse the product.[51]

With a heavy marketing campaign, OxyContin was promoted as the breakthrough drug in the treatment of moderate to severe pain. It was known as the "pharmaceutical heroin," as it gave a heroin-like euphoria. Patients with addiction to narcotic analgesics presented fake complaints to physicians, who, enthralled by Purdue's relentless marketing, freely wrote prescriptions for OxyContin. Priced substantially lower than street heroin, OxyContin gained the reputation as the poor man's heroin, hillbilly heroin, Oxy, OC, or OxyCotton, and transcended from being a miracle drug used for chronic analgesia to becoming one of the most highly abused and addictive drugs.

While being aggressively marketed and highly promoted, sales of OxyContin grew from $48 million in 1996 to almost $1.1 billion in 2000. The easy availability and high-pressure marketing of the drug spurred increased abuse, diversion, and addiction, and by 2004 OxyContin had become a leading drug of abuse in the United States.

The real crime is that according to the US Department of Justice, Purdue Pharma quickly discovered that OxyContin was both addictive and extremely popular among drug abusers. As *The New York Times* reported, as early as 1999, "company officials had received reports that the pills were being crushed and snorted; stolen from pharmacies; and that some doctors were being charged with selling prescriptions." They knew about the black market for the pills, and one Purdue executive described "OxyContin as the hottest thing on the street—forget Vicodin."[52]

Federal prosecutors charged that despite these reports, Purdue continued to insist it was less addictive and maintained its high-pressure marketing campaign.

By March 2016, March 2016, the FDA and Centers for Disease Control and Prevention (CDC) had started taking steps to address the opioid abuse epidemic. CDC director Dr. Tom Frieden wrote in the *New England Journal of Medicine* that while there wasn't enough data about long-term use of prescription opioids, "We know of no other medication routinely used for a nonfatal condition that kills patients so frequently."[53]

While death statistics for OxyContin specifically aren't available, by 2020, according to a study by the National Center for Health Statistics, a division of the CDC, a total of 932,364 people died in the U.S. from fatal opioid overdoses from 1999 through 2020. Another 106,000 were reported in 2021, pushing the total to over one million.[54]

In 2018, multiple members of the Raymond and Mortimer Sackler families, which controlled Purdue Pharma, were all named as defendants in suits filed by numerous states over their involvement in the opioid crisis. The following year, Purdue Pharma filed for Chapter 11 bankruptcy to address its debts, nearly all of which stemmed from thousands of lawsuits alleging that OxyContin helped kickstart the opioid epidemic. Purdue stated that its bankruptcy settlement, approved by a U.S. bankruptcy judge in 2021, would provide $10 billion in value to its creditors, including individual victims of addiction, hospitals, state and local governments, and other plaintiffs. But the Sackler family would have been immunized against lawsuits, and in 2023 the U.S. Department of Justice challenged that provision. The U.S. Supreme Court agreed to block the settlement until it could hear the case later in the year. What's more, according to the government, Sackler family members had siphoned $11 billion from Purdue before agreeing to contribute $6 billion to its opioid settlement.[55]

Shady Supplements

The vast universe of dietary supplements is composed of three types or categories:

1. The supplements that are healthy, wholesome, and provide you with nutrients that you may not be getting in your regular diet. When compared with "real food" on a price-per-pound basis, all supplements tend to be extremely expensive, but if you consume them wisely, they can be beneficial.

2. The supplements that provide minimal nutrition and are primarily effective because of the power of the placebo. In other words, if you take an expensive sugar pill and

you *believe* it will make you feel better, the odds are good that you *will* feel better. Call it mind over matter. Of course, you could also tell yourself that by drinking a glass of water you'll feel better, and if you believe it will have that effect, you'll be rewarded, and at far lower cost.

3. The supplements that, regardless of the legitimacy of some of their ingredients, contain toxins or other impurities that can make you sick. These are bad, and inexplicable. The business model of the global supplements industry is based on repeat customers. That is, most people who take supplements do so on a regular basis over months or even years. That's where the money is! If they think a supplement is helping them, they don't dare stop taking it! No! They become psychologically addicted, and the minute one bottle has been consumed, to continue feeling good they order another one. So it would be crazy for any manufacturer of supplements to include any substance that would make a loyal customer sick.

Nevertheless, supplements are manufactured products, and makers put stuff in them for various reasons. Here are six toxic substances that you may see if you read the label carefully.

These six toxic ingredients are just some of the common additives in many supplements that you should look out for:

Titanium dioxide—used as a filler to whiten products.

Magnesium silicate—added to the coatings of white pills and tablets.

Hydrogenated oil—used as a filler.

Coloring: Red 40, Blue 2, Yellow 5—artificial dyes linked to various diseases.

Artificial flavors and "natural" flavors—often in the form of high-fructose corn syrup, hydrolyzed vegetable protein, artificial sweeteners, and chemical flavor enhancers.

Lead, mercury, and PCBs—can be found in fish and therefore in fish oil.

To be safe, buy from a reputable company, avoid anything coming from China, and read the label carefully!

Marketing Strategies

In marketing their products, the makers of supplements need to convince you, the consumer, that you should take them. The question is, how can they do this? Because they are not drugs, the manufacturer cannot claim that they cure a disease. For example, vitamin C can actually prevent the disease scurvy. Iodine added to salt can prevent thyroid disease. But you never see ads for these outcomes. You just can't do it. But manufacturers can certainly claim that you might feel better if you take them.

As for regulation of dietary supplements, in the United States, the Federal Trade Commission (FTC) and the Food and Drug Administration (FDA) share responsibility under a long-standing liaison agreement between the two agencies. The FDA has primary responsibility for claims on *product labeling*, including packaging, inserts, and other promotional materials distributed at the point of sale. The FTC has primary responsibility for claims in *advertising,* including print and broadcast ads, infomercials, catalogs, and similar direct marketing materials.

In this chapter, we'll focus on the FTC and marketing. The FTC's truth-in-advertising law can be summarized in two common-sense propositions:
1. Advertising must be truthful and not misleading; and
2. Before disseminating an ad, advertisers must have adequate substantiation for all objective product claims conveyed, expressly or by implication, to consumers acting reasonably.[56]

These are fairly vague standards, as we'll see.

Brain Pills and Prevagen

As the massive Baby Boomer generation ages, a new opportunity has exploded in size: the market for pills and supplements that claim to enhance or preserve mental functioning among elderly people. It's an especially potent market because researchers have found almost 10 percent of U.S. adults ages 65 and older have dementia, while another 22 percent have mild cognitive impairment. For many types of dementia including Alzheimer's disease, there is no cure. You get it, and eventually it will kill you.

Millions of Boomers are terrified of dementia, and will do anything to avoid it.

Enter the brain pills. But they cannot claim to cure or prevent dementia. Most of them have no clinical trial evidence of efficacy in anything. But they can legally make limited claims about ingredients and with consumer testimony.

One of the very first brain pills was Prevagen. Its "active ingredient" is apoaequorin, the protein portion of aequorin, which is found in, among other creatures, jellyfish. To this day, the Prevagen TV ads feature glowing jellyfish.

That claim alone should make you laugh. Why? As they teach you in Biology 101, when you ingest *any* type of protein—cow, soybean, jellyfish—your digestive system tears it down into its ubiquitous amino acid components. There are 20 amino acids that your body uses to build its own proprietary proteins. Your proteins are DNA encoded for you alone. Your body does not care where the source protein comes from—lion or mouse, shark or jellyfish. They're all made from the same amino acids. Here's the bottom line: Because they are broken down into amino acids, the magical jellyfish proteins cannot cross the blood-brain barrier to reach the brain or affect its functioning.

The Federal Trade Commission took notice. In January 2017, the FTC and the Attorney General of New York State charged Quincy Bioscience, the maker of Prevagen, with making false and unsubstantiated claims about the supplement. The following year, the AARP Foundation filed a brief supporting the New York suit. A January 2019 JAMA article, co-authored by Joanna Hellmuth, a neurologist at the University of California San Francisco (UCSF) Memory and Aging Center, titled "The Rise of Pseudomedicine for Dementia and Brain Health," criticized Quincy for citing studies that lack "sufficient participant characterization and treatment randomization, and fail to include limitations."[57]

In 2020, Quincy Bioscience settled the case with the FTC that allowed the company to continue marketing Prevagen provided it qualified its advertising claims with a court-approved disclaimer. The TV ads continued to run at full throttle, with Prevagen claiming it could "improve short-term memory."

Here's the twist: Is Prevagen safe, as the company claims?

Sure it's safe! It won't hurt you any more than a sugar pill placebo will hurt you. But priced up to $70 per bottle, it's an awfully expensive way to fool yourself into believing you're benefiting from it.

As they say, *caveat emptor*—buyer beware!

Balance of Nature's "Fruits & Veggies"

The traditional method for advertising a drug or supplement has been to identify the problem the product will solve ("Soothes sore throat pain," etc.), and then cite third-party evidence that the product works as intended. Generally, such evidence takes the form of a clinical study. Manufacturers often say things like, "Studies have shown that Acme Diet Pills are safe and effective in helping you lose weight," or, "A clinical trial resulted in 50 percent clearer skin after using Suzy's Face Wipes." This has always been the way, and this approach gives the FTC and FDA an opportunity to demand the advertiser prove the claims are valid.

This is exactly what got Prevagen into trouble. In an extensive nationwide advertising campaign, Quincy Bioscience made the claim that the supplement was "clinically shown to improve memory." In response, the FTC and State of New York alleged that the company's own study found that Prevagen was no more effective than a placebo at improving memory. In effect, they charged that Quincy Bioscience had simply lied about their clinical trial.

In February 2019, the United States Court of Appeals for the Second Circuit ruled in favor of the FTC and remanded the case back to the district court for continuation of the litigation. The appellate court held that the "FTC has stated a plausible claim that [the defendants'] representations about Prevagen are contradicted by the results of [their] clinical trial and are thus materially deceptive."[58]

Another maker of supplements found a way to avoid that type of confrontation with authorities.

Founded in 1997 by Douglas Howard, a doctor of chiropractic, Balance of Nature is a health supplement company that offers fruit, vegetable, and spice supplements, most often seen on television as "Fruits & Veggies" in matching green and red bottles. The pills contain freeze-dried fruits and vegetables that have been ground into a fine powder, with nothing else added. The company claims the ingredients are third-party tested for potentially harmful substances such as pesticides, but no lab test results are published.

At first, Evig LLC—the parent company of Balance of Nature—did the usual thing and made unverified claims about the efficacy of the product. On August 20, 2019, the FDA sent Evig LLC a sternly worded "warning letter" about its practices. The letter read in part,

"From the video posted to your YouTube channel, 'How to Help Overcome Relapsing MS':

"The name of the video constitutes a claim that your products are intended for use in the cure, mitigation, treatment, or prevention of Multiple Sclerosis (MS).

"From the video description: 'Marie explains her daughter's situation with MS and how Balance of Nature's Fruits and Veggies have helped her with the energy and strength to fight her condition. Please share this with people you know fighting this same condition. . . Balance of Nature will give you over 10 servings of fruits and vegetables every day. The American Institute for Cancer Research and the USDA have confirmed that eating 9 to 11 servings of fruits and vegetables every day is the key to preventing cancer and other lifestyle diseases.'"

The FDA found this claim, and others, to warrant categorizing the products as drugs that could not be safely self-administered by the customer:

"Your products Whole Food Fruits, Whole Food Veggies, and Whole Food Fiber & Spice are intended for treatment of one or more diseases that are not amenable to self-diagnosis or treatment without the supervision of a licensed practitioner. Therefore, it is impossible to write adequate directions for a layperson to use your products safely for their intended purposes."[59]

In July 2023, following a consumer protection lawsuit filed by prosecutors in the California Food, Drug and Medical Device Task Force, Balance of Nature agreed to pay a settlement of $1.1 million for false advertising claims made surrounding its dietary supplements. The judgment called for any California resident who had purchased a Balance of Nature product in the previous six years to receive a notice on how to claim a refund from the restitution fund. The company was prohibited from engaging in the false advertising described in the complaint.

"The truth can be a hard pill to swallow," District Attorney Jeff Rosen said. "This company was dishonest in selling its products to the public. We will fight to make sure companies tell the truth to protect the health and welfare of our citizens."[60]

This was serious stuff—but Balance of Nature figured out how to play the game. In their flood of post-Covid era TV advertisements, the company featured testimonials from a variety of ordinary-looking senior citizens, each carefully stating how the pills made them *feel*. They said things like, "I've never had more energy," "My memory seems more sharp," or "I feel like a kid again. I'll always take Balance of Nature!" In other words, the company had learned to make no claims about curing disease or improving health. Instead, the claims from the spokespeople were always very narrow: "When I take Balance of Nature, I *feel* better."

Who could argue with that? The FDA and FTC cannot say, "You, the actor giving the testimonial, are lying about how the pills made you feel." It's common knowledge that a placebo—a sugar pill—has the power to make you feel better. It's a purely subjective response.

You would think that a TV ad with such weak claims for a supplement would be uncompetitive. After all, the pills cost over $30 a bottle, and you're urged to take two or three pills at a time. (They're just dried fruits and vegetables, so you could theoretically guzzle the entire bottle if you wanted to!) The product is not cheap. The net weight is not listed on the bottle, but let's say the contents of each bottle weighs half a pound. (We're being very generous here.) That means you're paying $60 per pound for freeze-dried versions of fresh vegetables you could buy at the grocery store for anywhere from $2 to $6 per pound. Of course, as a consumer you have that choice—you are free to pay the premium if you choose.

What's the secret to the success of Balance of Nature? The company has zeroed in on a vulnerable constituency: aging Baby Boomers who are terrified of getting old. The advertisements show a succession of happy senior citizens riding bicycles and playing tennis, then lovingly clutching their green and red bottles as they say how much energy they have. No clinical trials are even mentioned. They don't have to. The subliminal message is, "Why take a chance? Just like Balance of Nature helps these other people feel good, it can help *you* to feel better about aging. Don't be foolish and pass up something that could benefit you. Take the pills and be happy." Weirdly, the less they promise, the more compelling the message. And that proves that at the end of the day, people are less concerned about measurable, scientific results than they are about feeling good and being happy—even if it comes from an expensive pill.

As a consumer, you are free to choose how you spend your money. But unless you have cash to burn, you owe it to yourself to think hard about what marketing messages tell you—and what they *don't* tell you.

Phenylephrine, the Phantom Decongestant

As this book was being written, a new scandal was erupting in the news, involving over-the-counter remedies for nasal congestion from the common cold.

As Reuters reported on September 14, 2023, the U.S. Food and Drug Administration issued a ruling against three big healthcare companies—Procter & Gamble, Walgreens, and Johnson & Johnson Consumer, which is distinct from Johnson & Johnson, and is now known as Kenvue, an independent and publicly traded company. They were accused of deceiving consumers about cold decongestants containing an ingredient, phenylephrine, that an FDA advisory panel had unanimously declared ineffective. The class action lawsuits were filed after the panel reviewed several studies and concluded that the ingredient marketed as a decongestant was essentially no better than a placebo.

The FDA's decision carried a qualification—experts said the ingredient worked in nasal sprays, but not when taken orally in pill or liquid form.

"There's a serious problem when a 'decongestant' doesn't 'decongest,'" said Adam Levitt, founding partner of DiCello Levitt, the law firm that filed the first class action suit. "The FDA's recent findings are a prime example of how the pharmaceutical industry makes billions by knowingly selling questionable products to consumers who are suffering from specific ailments. Particularly in the years following the pandemic, the pharmaceutical industry's cynical willingness to peddle bogus cold and flu medication is deeply troubling."[61]

Phenylephrine has been listed in more than 250 commonly sold drugs for congestion including some versions of DayQuil, Sudafed, Tylenol, and Theraflu. The FDA asserted that about 242 million units of products containing phenylephrine were sold in the United States in 2022, generating $1.76 billion in sales and accounting for about four-fifths of the market for oral decongestants. As far back as 2018, said the FDA, Johnson & Johnson Consumer and Procter & Gamble should have known that their marketing claims about products with phenylephrine were "false and deceptive."

Similar lawsuits were filed against GlaxoSmithKline (GSK), which makes TheraFlu; and Reckitt Benckiser, which makes Mucinex Sinus Max. Walgreens, the big retail pharmacy chain, was sued because it produces and sells generic decongestants with the same ingredient.

The FDA did not seek to ban phenylephrine, which appears to be harmless, but said it would seek public opinion before finalizing its decision to remove it from the agency's list of ingredients for over-the-counter (OTC) use.[62]

The wheels of federal regulation often turn very slowly. As far back as 1993, Dr. Leslie Hendeles had published his first critique of phenylephrine, stating that when taken orally, it was destroyed by digestive chemicals in the stomach. That meant most of the medication didn't make it to the bloodstream, much less to the tissues in the congested nose.

For drugmakers, part of the attraction of phenylephrine was the fact that a decongestant proven to be effective, pseudoephedrine, had been severely restricted by the FDA because it was being used by illegal meth labs as an ingredient in black market methamphetamines. To curtail bootleg production of methamphetamine, in 2005 Congress passed the Combat Methamphetamine Epidemic Act, requiring pharmacies to keep logs of purchases of products containing pseudoephedrine and limiting the amount of those products an individual could purchase per day.

A third decongestant had been pulled from the market after being linked to high rates of strokes.

That left phenylephrine, which apparently worked only when applied though the nose. But the drug companies needed to protect their brands and profits on their oral medications, so when pseudoephedrine was taken out, phenylephrine was put in—and most consumers never knew the difference.

Chapter Six
Healthy Alternatives and Resources

We hope that reading this far into the book hasn't made you hopelessly depressed! In the first four chapters, it was our goal to alert you to the hazards in the road, so to speak. To be forewarned is to be forearmed. To defeat the enemy, you must first know him and what he can do. When it comes to your diet and the products you use on your body and in your home, ignorance is not bliss.

The ultimate purpose of this book is to show you the open road ahead, with opportunities for clean living, good health, and true happiness. We live in an era of unprecedented knowledge of how to eat and live free of the toxins and stuff you don't want. We have available to us a wealth of products and services that can support a healthy lifestyle.

Let's take a tour and see what we can find!

Food Marketing and Labeling

Food is super-important because it goes inside of you and literally becomes a part of you. The cheeseburger you eat will literally be broken down and re-formed into your muscles and other cells. The drugs you take will end up inside your brain. Those blueberries will help you see and hear. The sugar from that donut will, if it's more than you need to function at that moment, be stored as fat. Toxins and other junk? Well, if you ingest them, your body has to deal with them, which is not always easy.

When you buy fresh food at the supermarket, you only have two ways to evaluate its quality: your own senses (by looking at it and handling it) and the information provided to you by the seller (the label). But many of the toxins and impurities in food are invisible—you cannot see or smell them. Therefore, you must depend on statements made by the seller.

We can almost hear you laughing! Of course, sellers are notorious liars. (Sorry, but it's true.) Some are scrupulously honest, but many will tell you anything to make the sale. This is where the government enters the scene. The government—federal, mostly, because it involves interstate commerce—tries to level the playing field by making certain practices illegal and by insisting that sellers tell the truth about their products.

That's good, but it depends on how you define "the truth." We've seen this played out with products such as Prevagen and Balance of Nature, where it seems the business model is, "We tell the truth*"—with an asterisk that leads to a lot of fine print!

Let's tackle one important issue that's a common point of confusion in the produce and meat aisles: The use of the terms "organic," "all natural," "clean," and many others used to describe how plants and meat products have been grown and processed.

Here we go down the rabbit hole!

Clean. This term has no legal definition—it is defined by consumers. Generally, "clean eating" refers to consuming foods that are as close to their natural state as possible, hopefully organic, and most likely with minimal use of chemical additives and preservatives. In a survey by the Harvard School of Public Health, nearly half of the respondents considered themselves to be "clean eaters," with the most cited definitions being, "eating foods that aren't highly processed," "eating fresh produce," "eating organic foods," and "eating foods with a simple ingredients list."[63]

In response to the idea of "clean" eating, some people have embraced a vague dietary categorization of "dirty" eating, which is bad for you. They advise eliminating entire groups of foods including dairy, wheat, and refined sugars. So-called dirty foods have a higher fat and carbohydrate content, often from sugars and trans or hydrogenated fats, and are processed, packaged, and contain many ingredients. If this helps you, then go with it!

Natural. This term is quite vague and useless. The FDA has a limited definition of "natural," which is: "The FDA has considered the term 'natural' to mean that nothing artificial or synthetic (including all color additives regardless of source) has been included in, or has been added to, a food that would not normally be expected to be in that food." But this definition does not address food production methods, such as the use of pesticides, or food processing or manufacturing methods, such as thermal technologies, pasteurization, or irradiation.[64]

It's worth noting that foods containing naturally derived flavors, sweeteners, or other plant-based substances can be labeled "natural." Foods containing highly processed high fructose corn syrup (HFCS) can be labeled "natural," because the synthetic materials used to produce HFCS are not incorporated into the final product. And foods containing genetically engineered or modified ingredients can be labeled "natural."

For meat products, "natural" does not necessarily mean hormone-free or antibiotic-free; these are separate labels, also regulated by the United States Department of Agriculture (USDA).

Many products try to sneak in "not natural" ingredients, and many have been cited for it. They include:

- Blue Diamond Almond Milk—allegedly false for being labeled "all natural" while containing potassium citrate, a synthetic ingredient.
- Ben and Jerry's Ice Cream—allegedly marketed a product containing "Dutch" or alkalized cocoa as "all natural" despite the fact that the alkalized cocoa used is processed with potassium carbonate, a synthetic ingredient.
- Kellogg Co.'s Kashi branded snack foods and cereals, accused of bearing the false label "nothing artificial," while containing synthetic ingredients.[65]

There are many more! The USDA definition of "natural" is this: "A product containing no artificial ingredient or added color and is only minimally processed. Minimal processing means that the product was processed in a manner that does not fundamentally alter the product. The label must include a statement explaining the meaning of the term natural (such as 'no artificial ingredients; minimally processed')."[66]

Organic. The Organic Foods Production Act of 1990 established federal standards for the production and handling of organic agricultural products. The Act authorized USDA to create the USDA National Organic Program (NOP), which is responsible for developing and enforcing the USDA organic regulations governing organically produced crops and livestock.

If you read the USDA website, you'll quickly see that the definition of "organic" is very complicated and covers many facets of food production. Generally, the USDA organic regulations describe organic agriculture as "the application of a set of cultural, biological, and mechanical practices that support the cycling of on-farm resources, promote ecological balance, and conserve biodiversity. These include maintaining or enhancing soil and water quality; conserving wetlands, woodlands, and wildlife; and avoiding use of synthetic fertilizers, sewage sludge, irradiation, and genetic engineering."[67]

There are four levels of "organic." They are:

100% Organic. All ingredients must be certified organic. Any processing aids, such as pectin or cornstarch, must be organic.

Organic. At least 95 percent organic ingredients. All ingredients except those specified as allowable on the "National List" must be certified organic. The National List portion of the USDA organic regulations stipulates what nonorganic substances may be used in organic production and handling. The list is organized according to three categories: crop, livestock, and handling (processing). Nonorganic ingredients allowed may be used up to a combined total of 5% (excluding salt and water).

Made with organic. At least 70 percent organic ingredients, excluding salt and water. The non-organic agricultural products still must be produced without excluded methods.

"Excluded methods" is a USDA category defined as: "A variety of methods used to genetically modify organisms or influence their growth and development by means that are not possible under natural conditions or processes and are not considered compatible with organic production. Such methods include cell fusion, microencapsulation and macroencapsulation, and recombinant DNA technology (including gene deletion, gene doubling, introducing a foreign gene, and changing the positions of genes when achieved by recombinant DNA technology). Such methods do *not* include the use of traditional breeding, conjugation, fermentation, hybridization, in vitro fertilization, or tissue culture."[68]

Specific organic ingredients. Multi-ingredient products with some, but less than 70 percent, certified organic content fall under this category. These products cannot display the USDA Organic Seal or use the word "organic" on the principal display panel. But in the ingredient list, they can list certified organic ingredients and their percentage.[69]

How reliable are these labels? To earn certification as organic, the USDA requires a five-step process the farm or distributor must complete:

1. The farm or business adopts organic practices, selects a USDA-accredited certifying agent, and submits an application and fees to the certifying agent. The application includes a detailed description of the operation to be certified; a history of substances applied to land during the previous three years; the names of the

173

organic products grown, raised, or processed; and a written Organic System Plan (OSP) describing the practices and substances to be used.

2. The certifying agent reviews the application to verify that practices comply with USDA organic regulations.

3. An inspector conducts an on-site inspection of the applicant's operation.

4. The certifying agent reviews the application and the inspector's report to determine if the applicant complies with the USDA organic regulations.

5. The certifying agent issues organic certificate.[70]

The certification process must be completed annually. The farm or handling facility may be located anywhere in the world. The certification applies to the facility as a whole and the list of organic products it produces, and not simply to one or another individual product.

Organic Meat Products

To earn the "organic" seal, USDA regulations require that farm animals are raised in living conditions accommodating their natural behaviors, such as the ability to graze on pasture; are fed 100 percent organic feed and forage; are raised on certified organic land meeting all organic crop production standards; and are not administered antibiotics or growth hormones.

They must be produced without genetic engineering, ionizing radiation, or sewage sludge. Prohibited feed substances include mammalian or avian byproducts or other prohibited feed ingredients such as urea, manure, or arsenic compounds.

They must be managed in a manner that conserves natural resources and biodiversity; raised per the National List; and overseen by a USDA National Organic Program authorized certifying agent, meeting all USDA organic regulations.

Generally, animals must be managed organically from the last third of gestation (mammals) or second day of life (poultry); allowed year-round access to the outdoors whenever weather permits; and raised per animal health and welfare standards.

Some drugs, including vaccines, pain medication, and dewormers (for dairy and breeder stock) are allowed.

The adherence to organic livestock farming and ranching practices provides benefits beyond the meat products themselves. By using manure as fertilizer or composting it to conserve nutrients, organic practices minimize impacts to the off-farm environment and reduce manure runoff. To maintain soil fertility and protect soil and water quality, organic farmers use sustainable practices including cover crops and crop rotation.

Is Organic Food More Expensive?

In a word, yes. The price differential varies significantly from product to product; a USDA survey found that retail price premiums for 17 organic foods ranged from 7 percent above the nonorganic price for spinach to 82 percent higher for eggs.

But the question is... How precious is your health?

Here's the scoop on price. There are five reasons that make organic food a bit pricier than regular mass-produced food.
1. The demand for organic food is greater than the supply.
2. Production costs for organic foods are typically higher because the greater diversity of products means economies of scale cannot be achieved. Organic farms produce smaller harvests per acre than conventional mechanized farms. The prices of materials used in organic farming far exceed the prices of synthetic, chemical, and GMO products used on conventional farms.
3. Higher labor costs inputs per unit of output. Organic farming relies more on traditional, labor-intensive tilling, planting, and harvesting methods.
4. It's an added expense for a farm to become certified organic and to maintain that certification.
5. The mandatory segregation of organic and conventional produce, especially for processing and transportation, results in higher costs. Because of relatively small

volumes, marketing and the distribution chain for organic products is less efficient and costs are higher.
6. Perhaps worst of all, it's politics. The federal government overwhelmingly subsidizes conventional agriculture over organic. Research conducted by the California Public Interest Research Group found that, "between 1995 and 2010, American taxpayers spent over $260 billion in agricultural subsidies, with most of these subsidies given to the largest farming operations in the United States. Worse, most subsidies were used to finance commodity crops such as corn and soybeans that are often processed into food additives like high fructose corn syrup and vegetable oil and then used in junk food."[71]

Should you buy everything organic? Many experts say you should pick and choose. Robert Paarlberg, associate in the Sustainability Science Program at the Harvard Kennedy School and at Weatherhead Center for International Affairs, argues that synthetic nitrogen fertilizers, for example, which are forbidden, are chemically identical to the acceptable organic varieties, and are much cheaper. He wrote in 2021, "The biggest weakness in the organic rule is absolutism. Cutting back on the use of manufactured fertilizer is frequently a good idea, but the idea of cutting back to zero is needlessly rigid and absolute. Quests for purity in food and farming are not as dangerous as they are in race or religion, but they are just as lacking in scientific justification, and the advocates can be just as exasperating."[72]

Many experts say you can save money and still eat healthy foods by buying conventional foods with thick skins, such as pineapples, avocados, melons, citrus fruits, and bananas. This is because pesticides don't penetrate the skin, which you don't eat anyway.

Some foods you should buy organic because in their conventional form, their skins, which you eat, are likely to be contaminated with pesticides. They include strawberries, apples, spinach, kale, nectarines, grapes, bell peppers, cherries, peaches, pears, blueberries, and green beans.

Water, Water, Everywhere…

People of a certain age can remember when water came in two varieties.

Municipal tap water. In America, until the early 20th century, public water supplies were sketchy at best. Cholera, typhoid fever, dysentery, hepatitis A and E, and many other bacterial, viral, and parasitic diseases were caused by pathogens transmitted via water supplies. For most of human history, this was a significant problem, especially in urban areas. One of the most famous outbreaks of waterborne disease was the cholera epidemic in London in 1854, during which tens of thousands of people died. A major source of the *V. cholera* bacteria was the notorious Broad Street Pump, which—as was later discovered—had been polluted by a nearby cesspit that had begun to leak fecal bacteria.

At the beginning of the 20th century, with new scientific knowledge of bacteria, an immensely important public health challenge became the improvement and safety of drinking water quality, aiming to significantly reduce illness and death caused by contaminated drinking water. In 1908, Jersey City, New Jersey was the first city in the United States to begin routine disinfection of community drinking water. Over the next decade, thousands of cities and towns across the United States began disinfecting their drinking water, contributing to a dramatic decrease in communicable infectious diseases across the country. As the century progressed, the public's trust in safe drinking water led to the installation of millions of public drinking fountains (or "bubblers") in schools, retail stores, meeting places, airports, bus stations—anywhere people congregated.

Premium mineral water. Since the dawn of time, humans have recognized the health benefits of spring water with a high mineral content, not only for drinking but bathing as well. Popular in ancient Rome, mineral waters began to re-emerge in the late Renaissance. The commercial bottling of natural mineral waters first began in Europe in the mid 16th century, with mineral water from Vichy in France, Spa in Belgium, Ferrarelle in Italy, and Apollinaris in Germany. These were premium waters that rich folks would consume at home or in high-end restaurants.

Until the late 20th century, that's pretty much how you consumed water: Either from the tap or an expensive, luxury bottle you bought at a pharmacy.

Then in 1977, Perrier launched a successful advertising campaign in the United States, spearheading a resurgence in popularity for bottled water. Perrier's advertising was aimed at affluent baby boomers, born between 1945 and 1965, as they entered adulthood. The image was sophisticated, classy, and conscientious.

"It was a sophisticated way to go to a cocktail party and not drink alcohol," said Gary Hemphill, the director of research at the Beverage Marketing Corporation.

"It fairly sparkles with snobby cachet," *People* magazine declared of Perrier in 1978.

Perrier sought to link its name with physical fitness. In November 1977, shortly after its TV ads began flooding the airwaves, Perrier sponsored the New York City Marathon.

As Priceonomics.com reported, the campaign was a smashing success: In 1975, Americans bought 2.5 million bottles of Perrier. Just three years later, the company posted annual sales of 75 million bottles, and it soon hit 300 million bottles.[73]

With the rise of obesity, consumers began to abandon sugary soft drinks. Conflicts over fluoridation of public water and its safety convinced many that they needed to consume bottled water. That, and the astounding success of Perrier, opened the floodgates (so to speak).

Like any large beverage company, PepsiCo already had the infrastructure to purify and sell tap water. In 1994, it spent $3 million to install equipment at a plant in Wichita, Kansas, and then introduced Aquafina there, before rolling it out nationwide three years later. Aquafina was not spring water; it was just ordinary tap water given extra purification. In April 1999, Coca-Cola came out with Dasani, using the same water it used to make its soft drinks. It promoted Dasani by linking it with health and fitness. Yes, it was just high-class tap water—but you'd *feel good* when you bought it! These campaigns worked, and by 2013, purified tap water constituted more than half of the bottled water market.

Does bottled water *taste better* than tap water? Research studies have shown that most consumers cannot tell the difference![74]

If you really want to pay more for glorified tap water in a bottle and a fancy label, then go for it. But there's a serious issue here—the packaging.

Most commercial bottled water comes in single-use plastic bottles. According to a 2023 report from the United Nations University Institute for Water, Environment and Health, more than 1 million bottles of water are sold *every minute* around the world, and global sales of bottled water are expected to nearly double by 2030. The industry's enormous global success comes at a huge environmental, climate, and social cost.

The world annually generates around 600 billion plastic bottles, amounting to approximately 25 million tonnes of plastic waste, which is not recycled but is disposed of in landfills or as unregulated waste. Even more insidious—and potentially disastrous—is the fact that in developing nations ("the Global South"), the massive distribution of bottled water from private industry distracts from the more urgent task of building public water infrastructures that are desperately needed. Estimates suggest that less than half of what the world pays for bottled water annually would be sufficient to ensure clean tap water access for hundreds of millions of people for years to come.[75]

But how about your health?

Many people want to be thrifty and re-use plastic water bottles. This is because they know that single-use plastic water bottles cannot be recycled. As a Greenpeace report revealed, despite the widespread use of "recycling" symbols and marketing aimed at convincing us that it's okay to use throwaway plastic, only plastic #1 and #2 bottles and jugs meet the minimum legal standard to be labeled recyclable. Most of those plastic items you are encouraged to recycle—the ones numbered #3, #4, #5, #6, or #7—end up in landfills or incinerators, or polluting the environment.[76]

But the more use a disposable bottle gets, the more chemicals and toxins leach out of the plastic into the water. Over time harmful, carcinogenic substances like Bisphenol A (BPA) and Bis(2-ethylhexyl) phthalate (DEHP) can build up in your bloodstream and cause serious health problems.

The thermoplastic polyethylene terephthalate (PET) is the third most widely used type of plastic in food packaging, including in billions of single-use drinks bottles. PET is also known for being the source of potential chemical contaminants, including endocrine disruptors such as BPA, which can cause reproductive disorders, cardiovascular problems, and cancer, among other adverse effects.

The Challenge of Recycling

You can take action to both reduce your exposure to toxic chemicals in plastic water bottles and help with the growing problem of plastic in our environment. To start, you can just drink more tap water! The CDC says, "The United States has one of the safest and most reliable drinking water systems in the world. Every year, millions of people living in the United States get their tap water from a public community water system." The Environmental Protection Agency (EPA) is responsible for ensuring that public water supplies in America are safe. Every municipal water supplier must provide an annual report to its customers, known as a Consumer Confidence

Report (CCR). This report provides information on your local drinking water quality, including the water's source, contaminants found in the water, and how consumers can get involved in protecting drinking water. To find your local CCR, visit EPA's website.[77]

Unfortunately, high-profile disasters like the water crisis in Flint, Michigan can make people nervous, even when they live in areas with safe water. If you're skeptical of your tap water, get a home filter from Pur, Aquasana, AquaTru, Culligan, or Brita. Then buy a glass or aluminum bottle you can wash and refill. No more plastic! Problem solved!

If you want carbonated water, then get a device like a SodaStream to carbonate your water. They come with their own proprietary bottles, or you could transfer your fizzy drink into another bottle.

Some mineral waters come in glass bottles, which can be recycled. In fact, glass can be endlessly recycled with no loss of quality. New glass is made from four main ingredients: sand, soda ash, limestone and other additives for color or special treatments. Recycled glass is crushed, blended, and melted together with these starting materials. For every ton of glass recycled, more than a ton of raw materials are saved, including 1,300 pounds of sand, 410 pounds of soda ash, 380 pounds of limestone, and 160 pounds of feldspar.

Some types of glass cannot be recycled, including Pyrex and other types of heat-resistant glass, window glass, mirrors, crystal, and light bulbs. But any kind of glass used to make ordinary bottles can, and should, be recycled.

Aluminum is another infinitely recyclable material, and it takes up to 95 percent less energy to recycle it than to produce primary aluminum. This also saves toxic emissions including greenhouse gases. In fact, about 75 percent of all aluminum produced throughout history—nearly a billion tons—is still in use.

Steel is 100 percent recyclable, and be made into the same material of the same quality again and again. Same for tin, copper, and any other metal.

Here's a trivia question: In the United States, what is the most recycled material?

Answer: It's asphalt. Roads are torn up and the asphalt—made of aggregates, binders, and fillers—is endlessly recycled. The U.S. Environmental Protection Agency and the Federal Highway Administration report that about 90 million tons of asphalt pavement are reclaimed each year, over 80 percent of which is recycled.[78]

Why can't plastics be easily recycled? Because unlike steel, aluminum, and glass, plastics are made from hundreds of different resins. Different kinds of plastics can't be mixed together to be recycled. Even resins with the same number can't always be recycled together because of the way they're molded, which creates different chemical compounds.

Sadly, most of the plastic we throw into our recycling bins ends up in a landfill.

The solution? Buy less plastic. Period. Use glass or metal containers. If you must use plastic, look for the identification number. It's found within the little triangle with the "chasing arrows" design, molded into the bottom of nearly all plastic containers. Remember, the number is *not* a recycling symbol, but rather a plastic or resin identification code saying what type of plastic the item is made from. Generally, most recyclers will process plastics #1 and #2. Plastics #3 to #6 are more difficult to recycle, and some recycling centers do not accept them. Plastic #7 is even more difficult to recycle and is almost always excluded.

Here's a quick guide to what the numbers signify and the likelihood of the item being accepted for recycling.

1. **PET (Polyethylene terephthalate).** Soda and water bottles are the most common containers made out of PET. It can be recycled. Do not re-use plastic containers made of PET. It's meant for single-use applications, and repeated use may lead to leaching and bacterial growth. It's also difficult to clean or remove harmful chemicals, and may leach carcinogens. If you want to be really smart, avoid #1 PET bottles completely; but if you buy them, use them just once and then recycle.

2. **HDPE (High-density polyethylene).** It's used in a wide variety of applications including plastic bottles, shampoo bottles, bleach bottles, milk jugs, cutting

boards, and piping. HDPE meets FDA requirements for direct and indirect food contact, is resistant to hot water and cleaning chemicals, and will not absorb moisture, bacteria, or odors. It's very common, safe to use, and fully recyclable.

3. **PVC (Polyvinyl chloride).** Because it's soft and flexible, PVC is used in many applications including plastic food wrapping. Most recyclers will not take PVC products because the PVC is often contaminated with stabilizers and plasticizers, and plastics manufacturers believe that using virgin PVC resin is simply cheaper than recycling. You cannot include PVC waste in commercial recycling bins with everything else. You need to take it to a special plastics recycling facility to ensure it is being reused. Because PVC products contain toxins that leach throughout their entire life cycle, avoid reusing them, especially for food or for children's use..

4. **LDPE (Low-density polyethylene).** This is what most plastic bags, shrink wraps, and dry cleaner garment bags are made from. This stuff is bad for the

environment, and two leading causes of direct damage to wildlife are *entanglement* and *ingestion*. If exposed to consistent sunlight, they produce significant amounts of two greenhouse gases, methane and ethylene.

While most plastic bags are not recyclable, companies and recycling centers are seeking alternatives and, given their harmfulness to the environment, are researching how to recycle plastic bags. If recycled properly, LDPE is reusable and safe to repurpose.

5. **PP (Polypropylene).** This material is widely used in diverse products including fibers and filament, film, pipe, carpeting, packaging, automotive battery cases and automotive trim pieces, hinged packaging for commodity products (such as soap holders), toys, and bottle caps, and general commodity items. Polypropylene itself is recyclable, although many recyclers don't want it. One problem is that the polymer loses its strength and flexibility over successive recycling episodes. The bonds between the hydrogen and carbon in the compound become weaker, affecting

the quality of the material. This phenomenon is known as "downcycling." Many such plastics have to be mixed with virgin plastics and other materials to become valuable.

6. **PS (Polystyrene).** This is bad stuff. Styrene, a component of polystyrene, has been found in 100 percent of human fat tissue samples dating back to 1986. It is known to cause cancer in animals, and suspected to be both cancerous for humans as well.

There are different types of plastic #6.

Rigid plastic #6 is used to make items such as CD and DVD cases, plastic utensils, and plastic cups. It may be accepted in your curbside recycling cart.

Foam plastic #6 is a different material than rigid plastic #6, with different disposal requirements. Rigid plastic #6 is smooth and glossy, while foam plastic #6 is lightweight, porous, and dull. Commonly called Styrofoam, it's used for packing peanuts, take-out containers, disposable drinking cups, and more.

Polystyrene is generally not recyclable and accounts for about 35 percent of landfill material in the United States. Because it breaks apart so easily, it's often found inside the stomachs of marine animals and littering our beaches.

Avoid reusing polystyrene. Its chemical compounds have been linked with human health and reproductive system dysfunction. Polystyrene may leach styrene, a possible human carcinogen, into food products, especially when heated in a microwave.

7. **Polycarbonate, BPA, and Other Plastics.** This category includes a wide range of plastics with many different characteristics, including recyclable, non-recyclable, mixed plastics, and biodegradable plastics. Some examples are polycarbonates, polylactic acid (PLA), acrylonitrile butadiene styrene (ABS), acrylic, melamine, and nylon.

Assume that nothing with the #7 number can be recycled in your curbside service. Some #7 products, which include such varied products as Lego toy blocks, CDs, computer keyboards, and eyeglasses, can be recycled through specialty services.

Read your community guide to recycling, and follow the directions. Rinse off bottles and cans—no one wants food in the recycling bin. When someone puts unrecyclable stuff into the recycling stream, it adds to the cost of processing recycled material. Remember that non-crystal glass and metals including steel and aluminum are endlessly recyclable. The goal is to make the recycling industry profitable and attractive, so that it will grow!

Chapter Seven
Toward a Future of Clean Living

In the first six chapters of this book, we've focused exclusively on what you, as a consumer, can do to protect yourself from the multitudes of toxins that on a daily basis assault you from every direction.

The first step is awareness. Many toxins in our food and environment lurk out of sight, undetected, hidden from our five senses, and you have to learn about them in order to avoid them. This can be a challenging task, because product and food manufacturers often go to great lengths to conceal the true nature of the ingredients and processes they use, and supplements makers tend to exaggerate the therapeutic effects of their products.

The second step is action. Many people have an awareness of the toxicity of the products they buy, but just shrug and say, "What can you do?" They buy products with toxic ingredients because they think it's convenient or those products are cheaper than safe varieties. (This latter belief is usually not true.) But we cannot succumb to the false notion that "it doesn't matter." It does matter, because the choices we make every day have a cumulative effect on our health and our environment.

It's true that smoking just one cigarette won't harm you. The human body can deal with that single exposure to addictive toxins. But one cigarette after another, day after day, year after year, gradually overwhelms your body's defenses and opens the door to a host of deadly diseases including emphysema, cancer, and heart disease.

One doughnut won't kill you. But constantly overeating sugar and simple carbs can lead to obesity, which will shorten your life.

Sitting on the sofa and watching one game on TV won't make you sick. But being chronically inactive and not getting proper exercise day after day will increase your risk of many lifestyle diseases including diabetes.

Good habits lead to good health. Unhealthy habits lead to disease. That's just the way it is.

But it can be time-consuming to have to think about every product you buy, not only in terms of what it will do to your body but what the company itself is doing to society. What good does it do to buy organic asparagus if the company operating the farm mistreats the migrant workers who do the picking? Many companies try to ride the organic bandwagon because they see an opportunity for quick profits in an emerging market, not because they're truly dedicated to your good health.

Greenwashing

This recent phenomenon—companies pretending to be socially and environmentally conscious—is called "greenwashing."

Greenwashing is when a company spends more time and money on marketing itself as environmentally friendly than on actually improving its environmental record. It's a misleading marketing strategy designed to exaggerate the company's environmentally friendly actions and pander to consumers who prefer to buy goods and services from environmentally conscious brands.

Historically, one of the biggest and most notorious examples of corporate greenwashing was the deliberate effort by the world's biggest automaker, Volkswagen A.G., to circumvent federal emissions standards for diesel engine vehicles while promoting itself as an environmentally progressive company.

Here's what happened. The Environmental Protection Agency (EPA) sets standards for emissions—pollution—produced by all motor vehicles, including those powered by diesel engines. In addition, the state of California has its own standards, and because it's basically a mini-nation with the world's fifth largest economy (behind Germany and before India), the standards set by California carry a lot of weight in the marketplace.

From 2009 to 2015, Volkswagen described its diesel engines in passenger cars as being as clean as or cleaner than US and California requirements, while providing good fuel economy and performance. Volkswagen touted its "clean diesel" technology as an answer to the problem of air pollution, and the low emissions levels of Volkswagen vehicles enabled the company to receive green car subsidies and tax exemptions in the United States. In particular, VW claimed to have solved the problem of high emissions of nitrogen oxide (NOx), a pollutant common to diesel engines.

In reality, VW engineers had designed and installed software that enabled their cars to adjust their engine performance to pass EPA emissions tests, and then revert to "performance" levels for the consumer.

Tests conducted by the EPA tend to be repetitive and predictable in their format. The software—every vehicle these days has extensive software built into it—detected when the vehicle was being tested by the EPA. This was because EPA test procedures were standardized, with defined periods for acceleration, cruising, braking, and so on, that could easily be recognized by the onboard computer. When the onboard computer recognized performance patterns coinciding with EPA tests, it commanded the engine and drive train to revert to "safe," low-emissions mode. Then when performance patterns (speed, braking, steering etc.) indicated normal everyday driving, the controls were lifted and the engine would revert back to its uncontrolled, high-pollution methods.

On September 18, 2015, the EPA served a Notice of Violation (NOV) of the Clean Air Act on Volkswagen Group alleging that Volkswagen and Audi automobiles equipped with 2-litre TDI diesel engines, and sold in the US between 2009 and 2015, had an emissions-compliance "defeat device" installed. The EPA ordered the recall of 482,000 vehicles. The "defeat device" was specially-written engine-management-unit firmware that detected "the position of the steering wheel, vehicle speed, the duration of the engine's operation, and barometric pressure" when positioned on an EPA dynamometer.[79]

In addition, on November 20, 2015, the EPA accused Volkswagen of fitting all 3.0-litre TDI diesel engines sold in the US from 2009 through 2015 with emissions-cheating software, in the form of "alternate exhaust control devices." Two months later, the US Department of Justice filed a complaint in a federal court against VW, alleging that the 3.0-litre diesel engines met the legal emission requirements only during testing conditions, while at "all other times, including during normal vehicle operation, the vehicles operate in a 'normal mode' that permits NOx emissions of up to nine times the federal standard."[80]

Volkswagen paid a substantial price for its deliberate deception. In the United States, on January 11, 2017, Volkswagen Group pleaded guilty to carrying out a years-long conspiracy to defraud the US government, and to obstructing a federal investigation. For rigging more than 500,000 vehicles with software to cheat pollution laws and lying to U.S. investigators about the nature of the conspiracy, Volkswagen Group agreed to pay a $2.8 billion criminal fine and $1.5 billion in civil penalties. In addition, six executives were criminally charged.

The company rebounded, and today, Volkswagen—which owns Audi, Porsche, Bentley, Lamborghini, Bugatti, and other brands—is the largest automaker in the world, with a reported revenue of approximately $300 billion in 2022.

Speaking of California, the state is often on the vanguard of health protection, and has adopted a set of laws aimed at preventing greenwashing. In 2008, the California Legislature banned the use of words including "biodegradable," "degradable," or "decomposable" in the labeling of plastic food or beverage containers. In October 2011, the state's attorney general filed a first-of-its-kind greenwashing lawsuit against three companies that allegedly made false and misleading claims by marketing plastic water bottles as "100 percent biodegradable and recyclable." The companies sued were Aquamantra, a bottled water company in Dana Point, CA; Balance Water, a bottled water company in West Orange, N.J.; and ENSO Plastics, a bottle maker based in Mesa, AZ. In 2012, the court approved settlements requiring the companies to:

1. Stop using the term "biodegradable" on the labels of plastic bottles.
2. Stop using plastic bottles containing organic additives that compromise the bottles' recyclability.
3. Remove biodegradable claims from all marketing materials.

4. Provide corrective notice with respect to prior "biodegradable" claims.
5. Pay penalties.

How Do You Decide to Embrace or Reject a Company?

Given the tension between companies that try to promote themselves as environmentally progressive and the various watchdog groups, including the government, that call them out when they see deception, what's a consumer to do? And in the larger picture, what's an investor to do? Millions of people have retirement accounts or pension funds, and these usually include holdings in stocks. This is a challenge for every investor, even the big guys like Warren Buffett, arguably the most successful stock picker in modern history.

Here's one story about Buffett and his partner, Charlie Munger, and their thoughts about investing in tobacco products. At the annual meeting of Berkshire Hathaway Inc. in 1994, Buffett said investments in tobacco were, "fraught with questions that relate to societal attitudes and those of the present administration. I would not like to have a significant percentage of my net worth invested in tobacco businesses. The economy of the business may be fine, but that doesn't mean it has a bright future."[81]

At the 1997 annual meeting, Buffett commented, "Probably the biggest seller of cigarettes in the United States is Walmart, but just because they're the biggest seller of everything. They're the biggest seller of Gillette products and they're huge. And you know, do I find that morally reprehensible? I don't. If we owned all of Walmart, we'd be selling cigarettes at Walmart. But other people might call it differently, and I wouldn't disagree with them."

Charlie Munger added this about an opportunity they had to invest in a company called Conwood, which made smokeless tobacco products including snuff and chewing tobacco: "You definitely are going to kill people with that product that have no reason to die. It's the best deal we ever saw, we couldn't lose money doing it and we passed... Do we miss the two or three billion dollars we would easily have had? Not an iota. We had a moment's regret? Not an iota. We were way better off not making a killing out of a product we knew going in was a killing product."[82]

These are interesting questions. Here are a few you can ask yourself—there are no right or wrong answers!

Would you....

- Buy a product that you knew was toxic to you personally or harmed the environment?
- Invest in a company that made one or more toxic or dangerous products, such as a manufacturer of firearms?
- Support a company that was anti-union and paid its workers poorly?
- Spend money in a big box store that, among thousands of ubiquitous products, sold a relatively small number of toxic products, like Walmart?
- Endorse a company like Nike that has been repeatedly accused of labor abuse at its factories in developing nations?

These can be difficult questions, but there are ways to begin to answer them.

Benefit Corporations

In our capitalist economy, most goods and services are created by corporations. A corporation is a group of people who have joined together to solve a problem, such as feeding people, making clothing for them, or getting them from one place to another. These owners pool their money to start the company, make the product or service, sell it, pay their suppliers, and then divide up the profits amongst themselves. These owners have two motivations: to do something good and useful for their fellow citizens, and to earn money for their own living expenses.

Over the years, many theoreticians have argued about the importance of making a profit versus all other considerations, such as doing good for the community. One of the leading voices for the pursuit of profits above all else was Milton Friedman, who burst to the forefront of public consciousness on September 13, 1970, with the publication in *The New York Times* of his article entitled, "A Friedman

Doctrine: The Social Responsibility of Business Is to Increase Its Profits."

Friedman insisted that the exclusive owners of a business are its shareowners—the people who contributed cash. Everyone else connected with the business is an employee, including the CEO, even if he or she is the founder. The managers of the business are therefore handling someone else's money, and are obliged to not waste it on frivolous "feel-good" activities that do not produce an immediate cash return on investment. He wrote that if a company engaged in any sort of activity designed to benefit the community and not simply sell more products, then, "In each of these cases, the corporate executive would be spending someone else's money for a general social interest. Insofar as his actions in accord with his 'social responsibility' reduce returns to stockholders, he is spending their money. Insofar as his actions raise the price to customers, he is spending the customers' money. Insofar as his actions lower the wages of some employees, he is spending their money."[83]

So if a company makes cigarettes, and cigarettes are legal, then the company must always strive to sell more cigarettes and deliver more profits to the shareholders.

Every company has a charter, which states the activities of the company. Shareholders can sue the board of directors if it appears the company is not pursuing its charter or articles of incorporation. If a guy like Milton Friedman wants the owners of a company to focus solely on quarterly profits, and believes the owners are too concerned with acting in the best interests of the employees, or of the community, he can sue them.

This is why the structure known as a benefit corporation was invented. A benefit corporation is the same as any other, except that its articles of incorporation includes specific language stating the company may use a variety of criteria to gauge success, including profits but also things like addressing social, economic, and environmental needs of the community within which it operates. This puts potential investors on notice that if they buy shares in the company, they cannot sue if, for example, the company takes on the expense of training workers with disabilities, or gives paid leaves of absence to new parents, or pays more for packaging that's truly recyclable.

Benefit corporation is a state, not federal, designation. In April 2010, Maryland became the first U.S. state to pass benefit corporation legislation. Since then, most other states have followed suit, but not all. Check with your local secretary of state to find out.

How can you find out if a company is not just a regular corporation but a benefit corporation? You can find lists online, such as on Wikipedia, or you can research their website or other company publications.

B-Corp Certification

In theory, a benefit corporation could be in the business of selling cigarettes or firearms. To take the concept to its logical conclusion and ensure that a "benefit" corporation was truly sincere about benefitting the community, in 2006, in Berwyn, Pennsylvania, Andrew Kassoy, Bart Houlahan, and Jay Coen Gilbert founded a non-profit organization called B Lab. It created, and awards, the B corporation certification for for-profit organizations.

The "B" stands for beneficial, and indicates that the certified organizations voluntarily meet certain standards of transparency, accountability, sustainability, and performance, with an aim to create value for society, not just for traditional stakeholders such as the shareholders. As B Lab says, "We're building the B Corp movement to change our economic system—and to do so, we must change the rules of the game. B Lab creates standards, policies, tools, and programs that shift the behavior, culture, and structural underpinnings of capitalism. We mobilize the B Corp community towards collective action to address society's most critical challenges."[84]

    Basically, the B Corps process is one of certification. B Corp Certification is a designation that a business meets established standards of verified performance, accountability, and transparency on a wide range of factors including employee benefits, charitable giving, supply chain practices, the environment, and input materials. In order to achieve certification, a company must:

- "Demonstrate high social and environmental performance by achieving a B Impact Assessment score of 80 or above and passing a risk review.
- "Make a legal commitment by changing their corporate governance structure to be accountable to all stakeholders, not just shareholders, and achieve benefit corporation status if available in their jurisdiction.
- "Exhibit transparency by allowing information about their performance measured against B Lab's standards to be publicly available on their B Corp profile on B Lab's website."[85]

B-Corp is not a legal status. The IRS does not care if you're a B Corp. It's a way to communicate to investors, customers, and any other stakeholders that your company strives to meet high standards while being held accountable.

You can find a list of certified B Corp companies at bcorporation.net as well as on many other websites.

Fair Trade Certification

Demand for sustainable and ethically-sourced products is continuing to rise, and consumers increasingly expect the brands they see in the stores to align with these values. But how does a consumer know the bananas, chocolate, or coffee they buy has been sourced from a reputable provider who rejects the use of toxins while treating their workers fairly?

The idea and practice of "fair trade" emerged after World War Two. One of the movement's key pioneers was an American businesswoman named Edna Ruth Byler. She felt empathy for the women artisans she encountered in Puerto Rico and, to help them earn a living, began selling their handmade textiles to her friends and neighbors. Out her efforts grew Ten Thousand Villages and a global fair trade movement spearheaded by various religious groups.

Over time, the independent fair trade organizations began to coalesce. In 1997, the worldwide Fairtrade Labelling Organizations International (FLO) association was established. In 1989, the International Federation of Alternative Trade (IFAT; later renamed World Fair Trade Organization) brought together 38 fair trade organizations under one roof. The following year, the European Fair Trade Association (EFTA) was formally established by 11 fair trade import organizations in nine European countries. In 1998, more groups came together to establish an informal working group called FINE, an acronym of the names of the member organizations. FINE was dedicated to increasing worldwide awareness of the fair trade movement through active campaigning in political circles and organizing public events.

Even today, the term "fair trade" is not specific to any one organization or certifying body. It's a global movement made up of a diverse network of advocates, companies, producers, shoppers, and organizations working together to build a more equitable model of trade.

In the United States and Canada, the Fair Trade Certified Mark is a fair trade certification mark you'll see most often. It's the North American equivalent of the International Fairtrade Certification Mark used in Europe, Africa, Asia, Australia and New Zealand. It appears on products as an independent guarantee that disadvantaged producers in the developing world are getting a fair deal.

For a product to carry either certification marks, it must come from Fair Trade USA inspected and certified producer organizations. The crops must be grown and harvested in accordance with the fair trade standards set by Fair Trade USA.

But what does this mean to you, the consumer?

While 60 percent of fair trade produce is organic, it's not a requirement. Fair trade farmers implement environmentally friendly farming practices, such as using non-GMO seeds and avoiding certain toxic pesticides. The Fair Trade label does not require organic certification because for some local farmers, barriers including cost, location, quality of soil, and training often make it difficult to pursue.

Are Fair Trade products more expensive? Sometimes no, sometimes yes—but usually only by pennies, which can make a huge difference to local farmers. As Peter Kettler, senior coffee manager at Fairtrade International, wrote in 2019, at that time Fairtrade certified coffee cooperatives earned the Fairtrade Minimum Price of $1.40 per pound (about 40 percent more than the current market price) or $1.70 per pound for organic beans. They could also earn 20 cents per pound in Fairtrade Premium, of which at least 25 percent is invested in productivity and quality initiatives. The problem is the pressure from big multinational coffee retailers—Starbucks, Dunkin', and Tim Hortons are the three largest coffee companies in the world—that suppress prices paid to farmers. While the global coffee industry now generates more than $200 billion per year, noted Kettler, the average farmer's income has not changed in the past 20 years, or has even declined when factoring increased costs of farming.[86]

Benefit corporations, certified B-Corps, and Fair trade are a time-tested way for you, the consumer, to choose the foods and products you buy with more certainty that you're buying a healthful and non-exploitative item!

Thank you for reading this book. We hope it will help you live a better, healthier life! If you want more information, please

About Authors
Dr Labib Ghulmiyyah

Dr. Ghulmiyyah is a maternal-fetal medicine specialist, obstetrician-gynecologist, researcher, educator, and advocate for environmental health in pregnancy and women's wellness. After earning his MD from the American University of Beirut, he completed his residency at Atlanta Medical Center followed by a fellowship in Maternal-Fetal Medicine at the University of Cincinnati and University of Texas Medical Branch.

Dr. Ghulmiyyah joined the faculty at the American University of Beirut, where he served as Head of Maternal-Fetal Medicine Division and the Residency Program Director, helping lead the program to ACGME-I accreditation.

After the tragic Beirut explosion and deteriorating situation, Dr. Ghulmiyyah made the difficult decision to relocate back to the United States, joining the faculty at the renowned University of Miami/Jackson Memorial Hospital as the Director of the Labor & Delivery Unit. He developed and served as Director of the Placenta Accreta Center of Excellence.

Currently, Dr. Ghulmiyyah is the Medical Director of Maternal Fetal Medicine at Pediatrix Medical Group, bringing over 20 years of clinical and academic experience. He is double board certified in Obstetrics & Gynecology and Maternal Fetal Medicine.

Beyond the clinic and hospital, Dr. Ghulmiyyah is a certified functional medicine practitioner and culinary coach. He is an acclaimed keynote speaker on managing exposure to toxicants during pregnancy and postpartum recovery. He is transforming mindsets around exposure to toxicants in pregnancy, helping mitigate risks through his educational initiatives and awareness campaigns.

Dr. Ghulmiyyah's clinical skills are matched only by his academic accomplishments and passion for illuminating the underlying causes of disease. He has shared his research on prominent platforms worldwide, authored textbooks and published extensively to push boundaries.Dr. Ghulmiyyah is dedicated to uncovering the root causes of disease through research and teaching the "why" behind medicine. By empowering mothers and families with knowledge, he aims to drive better outcomes. Dr. Ghulmiyyah's multifaceted approach showcases his commitment to advancing maternal fetal health.

Dr Rudolph Eberwein

Dr. Rudolph Eberwein was born and raised in the beautiful island of Haiti. During the early 1990's Haiti was going through some difficult political moments and things were extremely unstable. After attending first year of Medical School in Haiti, the civil unrest had become so unbearable, he decides to leave Haiti for America and pursue his academics abroad. He arrived in the United States at age 21 and although he was able to read and write English, he could not speak it. He worked several odd jobs until he felt he could communicate sufficiently. At this time, he began to pursue his academic goals of becoming a doctor once again. Dr. Rudy did his undergraduate studies at the University of Florida, where he earned a Bachelor of Science in Nutritional Science. He then attended the Miller School of Medicine at The University of Miami where he obtained his Medical Degree in 1998. Dr. Rudy completed his internship and residency in Internal Medicine in 2001 at University of Miami/Jackson Memorial Hospital. Dr. Eberwein obtained board certification in Internal Medicine in 2001 and started his career as a Hospitalist in several major hospitals in Virginia and Miami. There, he gained invaluable experience treating very sick patients in numerous departments. They included the Emergency Department, Intensive Care Unit, and the general medical wards. This demanding work gave Dr. Eberwein a strong insight and skill set to help him deal with his patients at their most vulnerable and difficult moments. In 2005, he co-founded A New You Weight Loss and Rejuvenation Center along with his wife Dr. Keisha Eberwein. They have helped thousands of patients become healthier and help prevent chronic debilitating diseases through their use of applied nutrition, behavioral modification, and hormone replacement. His areas of interest and expertise include Nutrition, Naturopathic Medicine, Age Management, Hormone Deficiencies, and Restorative Medicine. In 2007, he became the Medical Director of a major Nursing Home in Miami. He has been treating and following many patients with multiple medical issues including but not limited to Andropause, Menopause, Somatopause, Alzheimer's dementia, chronic degenerative diseases, cancer, poor quality of life scores, pain control, and end of life issues. Also, he obtained a board certification in Age Management Medicine with AMMG (Age Management Medicine Group) and continues to thrive and learn more in the area of medical health science. Dr. Eberwein has been happily married for 20 years. They have 14-year-old twin daughters. His hobbies include exercising, weight training, racquetball, reading, traveling, and just relaxing by the beach. He is a family man and always makes time for his very large immediate and extended family as well as countless friends. You will hear many people describe him as one of the nicest people you will ever want to meet. His positive attitude and infectious smile make you want to immediately spend more time with him and become his best friend. His bedside manner is impeccable. Dr. Rudy makes you feel comfortable in whatever situation you find yourself in.

Endnotes

[1] Drzyzga O. Diphenylamine and derivatives in the environment: a review. Chemosphere. 2003 Dec;53(8):809-18. doi: 10.1016/S0045-6535(03)00613-1. PMID: 14505701

[2] EPA.https://www3.epa.gov/pesticides/chem_search/reg_actions/reregistration/fs_PC-038501_10-Apr-98.pdf

Sd mjkio9 [3] CDC. https://www.cdc.gov/nchs/data/nvsr/nvsr50/nvsr50_16.pdf

[4] Robert H. Lustig, et al. Obesity I: Overview and molecular and biochemical mechanisms, Biochemical Pharmacology, Volume 199, 2022, 115012, ISSN 0006-2952.

[5] https://diabetesjournals.org/spectrum/article/15/2/109/459/Toxins-and-Diabetes-Mellitus-An-Environmental

[6] Pizzorno J. Is the Diabetes Epidemic Primarily Due to Toxins? Integr Med (Encinitas). 2016 Aug;15(4):8-17. PMID: 27574488; PMCID: PMC4991654.

[7] Reis J, Giroud M, Kokubo Y. Environmental Risk Factors for Stroke and Cardiovascular Disease. Encyclopedia of Cardiovascular Research and Medicine. 2018:238–47. doi: 10.1016/B978-0-12-809657-4.64111-X. Epub 2017 Nov 30. PMCID: PMC7150018.

[8] Yang SN, Hsieh CC, Kuo HF, Lee MS, Huang MY, Kuo CH, Hung CH. The effects of environmental toxins on allergic inflammation. Allergy Asthma Immunol Res. 2014 Nov;6(6):478-84. doi: 10.4168/aair.2014.6.6.478. Epub 2014 Oct 15. PMID: 25374746; PMCID: PMC4214967.

[9] https://www.medievalists.net/2022/05/pollution-medieval-cities/

[10] EPA. https://www.epa.gov/pmcourse/particle-pollution-exposure

[11] https://www.stateofglobalair.org/health/global#key-diseases

[12] EPA. https://cfpub.epa.gov/ncea/hfstudy/recordisplay.cfm?deid=332990

[13] Elaine L. Hill, Lala Ma. "Drinking water, fracking, and infant health." Journal of Health Economics, Volume 82, 2022, 102595, ISSN 0167-6296, https://doi.org/10.1016/j.jhealeco.2022.102595.

[14] https://www.vice.com/en/article/xd7qvn/the-town-erin-brockovich-rescued-is-now-almost-a-ghost-town-992

[15] NYT. https://www.nytimes.com/1990/10/22/nyregion/love-canal-suit-focuses-on-records-from-1940-s.html

[16]NYT. https://www.nytimes.com/1978/08/02/archives/upstate-waste-site-may-endanger-lives-abandoned-dump-in-niagara.html

[17] EPA. https://www.epa.gov/archive/epa/aboutepa/love-canal-tragedy.html

[18]https://chej.org/about-us/story/love-canal#:~:text=From%201974%20to%201978%2C%2056,authorities%20quickly%20dismissed%20the%20study.

[19] EPA. https://www.epa.gov/superfund/what-superfund

[20]TFF.https://toxicfreefuture.org/toxic-chemicals/persistent-bioaccumulative-and-toxic-chemicals-pbts/

[21] https://pubs.acs.org/doi/10.1021/acs.est.2c07247

[22] NYT. https://www.nytimes.com/2023/05/03/well/live/consumer-products-toxic-chemicals.html

[23]https://ysph.yale.edu/news-article/study-identifies-potentially-harmful-substances-in-household-dust/

[24]https://www.niehs.nih.gov/health/topics/agents/sya-bpa/index.cfm#:~:text=Bisphenol%20A%20can%20leach%20into,water%20bottles%2C%20and%20baby%20bottles.

[25] CDC https://www.atsdr.cdc.gov/pfas/health-effects/exposure.html

[26] https://www.consumerreports.org/health/food-contaminants/dangerous-pfas-chemicals-are-in-your-food-packaging-a3786252074/

[27] https://www.saferstates.com/toxic-chemicals/pfas/#:~:text=CA%2C%20CO%2C%20and%20MN%20are,to%20eliminate%20PFAS%20in%20cosmetics.

[28] https://www.jdsupra.com/legalnews/california-s-toxic-free-cosmetics-act-4502322/

[29] https://www.ewg.org/the-toxic-twelve-chemicals-and-contaminants-in-cosmetics

[30] GEF.org.https://www.thegef.org/sites/default/files/documents/2022-10/GEF_good_practice_brief_POPs_alternatives_India_2022_9_1.pdf

[31] FDA.https://www.fda.gov/food/ingredients-additives-gras-packaging-guidance-documents-regulatory-information/food-defect-levels-handbook

[32] FDA. https://mercuryfactsandfish.org/mercury-facts/the-fda-action-level/

[33] EPA.https://www.epa.gov/pesticide-science-and-assessing-pesticide-risks/human-health-issues-related-pesticides#:~:text=The%20health%20effects%20of%20pesticides,Some%20pesticides%20may%20be%20carcinogens.

[34] Robinson B. (1947). A Nutritionist Ponders the D.D.T. Problem. Private Publication (Report). St. Louis, Michigan.

[35] https://toxicfreefuture.org/toxic-chemicals/pcbs-and-ddt/#:~:text=We%20are%20still%20exposed%20to,and%20dairy%20products%20contain%20DDT.

[36] NPIC. http://npic.orst.edu/factsheets/glyphogen.html

[37] Drugwatch. https://www.drugwatch.com/roundup/

[38] Bayer. https://www.bayer.com/media/en-us/bayer-provides-update-on-path-to-closure-of-rounduptm-litigation/

[39] Harvard. https://sitn.hms.harvard.edu/flash/2015/roundup-ready-crops/

[40] https://worldpopulationreview.com/country-rankings/countries-that-ban-gmos

[41] http://gutenberg.net.au/ebooks07/0700461.txt

[42] https://jamanetwork.com/journals/jama/article-abstract/454402

[43] https://www.ncbi.nlm.nih.gov/pmc/articles/PMC1651180/?page=1

[44] https://pharmaceutical-journal.com/article/opinion/the-history-of-snake-oil

[45] FDA. https://www.fda.gov/food/information-consumers-using-dietary-supplements/questions-and-answers-dietary-supplements#:~:text=A%20dietary%20supplement%20is%20a,intended%20to%20supplement%20the%20diet.

[46] https://www.eatingwell.com/article/7922214/supplements-opss-scorecard/

[47] FDA. https://www.fda.gov/drugs/drug-approvals-and-databases/drugsfda-glossary-terms#M

[48] FDA. https://www.fda.gov/news-events/press-announcements/fda-approves-first-nonprescription-daily-oral-contraceptive

[49] FDA. https://www.fda.gov/drugs/frequently-asked-questions-popular-topics/prescription-drugs-and-over-counter-otc-drugs-questions-and-answers

[50] CNN. https://www.cnn.com/2016/05/12/health/opioid-addiction-history/index.html

[51] Gale A. Sacklers Sacked But Purdue Still Caused Opioid Epidemic. Mo Med. 2022 Mar-Apr;119(2):109. PMID: 36036027; PMCID: PMC9339402.

[52] NYT. https://www.nytimes.com/2018/05/29/health/purdue-opioids-oxycontin.html

[53] CNN. https://www.cnn.com/2016/05/12/health/opioid-addiction-history/index.html

[54] NIH.https://nida.nih.gov/research-topics/trends-statistics/overdose-death-rates#:~:text=Overall%2C%20drug%20overdose%20deaths%20rose,overdose%20deaths%20reported%20in%202021.

[55] Reuters.https://www.reuters.com/legal/us-supreme-court-scrutinize-purdue-pharma-bankruptcy-settlement-2023-08-10/

[56] https://www.ftc.gov/system/files/documents/plain-language/bus09-dietary-supplements-advertising-guide-industry.pdf

[57] https://www.beingpatient.com/prevagen-settlement/

[58] https://www.cspinet.org/case/prevagen#:~:text=In%20an%20extensive%20nationwide%20advertising,a%20placebo%20at%20improving%20memory.

[59] FDA.https://www.fda.gov/inspections-compliance-enforcement-and-criminal-investigations/warning-letters/evig-llc-dba-balance-nature-580888-08202019

[60] https://countyda.sccgov.org/news/news-release/supplement-company-pay-11-million-false-advertising-settlement

[61] https://dicellolevitt.com/pharmaceutical-companies-violated-consumer-protection-laws-committed-fraud-by-

selling-medicine-containing-ineffective-nasal-decongestant-according-to-new-lawsuit/

[62]Reuters.https://www.reuters.com/legal/jj-pg-sued-after-fda-panel-ruling-cold-medicine-decongestant-2023-09-14/

[63]https://www.hsph.harvard.edu/nutritionsource/clean-eating/#:~:text=Generally%2C%20clean%20eating%20is%20assumed,any%20chemical%20additives%20and%20preservatives.

[64] FDA. https://www.fda.gov/food/food-labeling-nutrition/use-term-natural-food-labeling

[65]https://www.gray-robinson.com/insights/post/1247/fda-next-action-on-defining-natural-for-food-labeling-purposes-remains-unclear

[66]USDA.https://ask.usda.gov/s/article/What-does-natural-meat-and-poultry-mean#:~:text=A%20product%20labeled%20%22natural%22%20is,not%20fundamentally%20alter%20the%20product.

[67] AMS / USDA. https://www.ams.usda.gov/publications/content/fact-sheet-introduction-organic-practices

[68]AMS/USDA.https://www.ams.usda.gov/sites/default/files/media/MSExcludedMethodsProposaFall2019.pdf

[69]USDA.https://www.usda.gov/media/blog/2016/07/22/understanding-usda-organic-

label#:~:text=There%20are%20four%20distinct%20labeling,100%20percent%20certified%20organic%20ingredients.

[70] AMS / USDA. https://www.ams.usda.gov/services/organic-certification/becoming-certified

[71] https://www.liveabout.com/reasons-organic-food-costs-more-2538165

[72] https://news.harvard.edu/gazette/story/2021/02/author-robert-paarlberg-argues-against-buying-organic/

[73] https://priceonomics.com/the-ad-campaign-that-convinced-americans-to-pay/#:~:text=Perrier's%20American%20transformation%20began%20with,%2419.7%20million%20in%20today's%20dollars.

[74] https://www.bu.edu/articles/2011/bottled-vs-tap-which-tastes-better

[75] https://inweh.unu.edu/global-bottled-water-industry-a-review-of-impacts-and-trends/

[76] https://www.greenpeace.org/usa/the-myth-of-single-use-plastic-and-recycling/

[77] CDC. https://www.cdc.gov/healthywater/drinking/drinking-water-faq.html#:~:text=The%20United%20States%20has%20one,water%20or%20ground%20water%20source.

[78] https://americanasphalt.com/how-is-asphalt-paving-recycled/#:~:text=Supporting%20data%20from%20the%20U.S.,percent%20of%20which%20is%20recycled.

[79] Grimmelmann, James (24 September 2015). "The VW Scandal Is Just the Beginning". Mother Jones. Retrieved 27 September 2015.

[80] "United States Files Complaint Against Volkswagen, Audi and Porsche for Alleged Clean Air Act Violations". US Dept of Justice. 4 January 2016. Retrieved 6 January 2016.

[81] https://www.industrydocuments.ucsf.edu/tobacco/docs/#id=ggkm0127

[82] https://invariant.substack.com/p/buffett-berkshire-tobacco

[83] NYT.https://www.nytimes.com/1970/09/13/archives/a-friedman-doctrine-the-social-responsibility-of-business-is-to.html

[84] B Lab. https://www.bcorporation.net/en-us/movement/about-b-lab/

[85] B Lab. https://www.bcorporation.net/en-us/certification/

[86] https://www.fairtradeamerica.org/news-insights/we-love-coffee-are-we-willing-to-pay-the-price/#:~:text=Fairtrade%20certified%20coffee%20cooper

atives%20currently,or%20%241.70%20per%20pound%20organic.

Made in the USA
Columbia, SC
25 May 2024

99ccf234-d9bb-4882-82e3-4f9bd593f7c2R01